Blessed EXPECTATIONS

Nine Months of Wonder, Reflection & Sweet Anticipation

JUDY FORD

CONARI PRESS
Berkeley, California

Conari Press books are distributed by Publishers Group West

Cover design: Nita Ybarra Design
Interior design: Suzanne Albertson
Cover photo: George Kamper / Tony Stone Images

ISBN: 1-57324-085-0

Library of Congress Cataloging-in-Publication Data

Ford, Judy. 1944-

Blessed expectations : nine months of wonder, reflection & sweet anticapation / Judy Ford.

p.   cm.
ISBN 1-57324-085-0 (trade paper)
1. Motherhood.   2. Pregnancy—Psychological aspects.
3. Childbirth—Psychological aspects.   4. Love, Maternal.   I. Title.
HQ759.F67   1997
306.874'3—dc21   96-52743
CIP

Printed in the United States of America on recycled paper
10 9 8 7 6 5 4 3 2 1

For babies everywhere

&

the mommies and daddies
who care for them.

Blessed Expectations

Preparing Heart and Soul for Your Baby xi

Sweet Anticipation

Reflection

Wonder

Preparing Heart and Soul for Your Baby

As gold passing through the fire
is shined to the highest radiance;
You polish my soul through pregnancy
so I become a mother filled
with wisdom, light, and love.

 hen you grasp that what you secretly suspected, hoped, and longed for is true—you're indeed going to have a baby—you're at once thrilled, flabber-gasted, weak in the knees. Even though you believed that you might be expecting—perhaps you carefully planned it—your thoughts are spinning. Slightly woozy, you need to sit down, yet you feel like dancing.

The positive confirmation turns the possibility that "I might be pregnant" into the heart stopping reality, "Oh my, now what will I do?" You're intoxicated by the freshness of the news and as it ebbs and flows; you're thrust into the actuality that a precious life is growing within you—in a matter of months you'll be a mother. And while you're floating on a cloud, enchanted by baby daydreams, you also want to come down to earth and get prepared.

So, chances are as soon as you heard you were pregnant (or maybe even before), you ran out and bought at least one book that focuses on what to expect now that you're expecting. You want to know what changes your body will be going through. There are many good resource books to show you the stages of development of the baby in your womb, books that give you sound prenatal advice as to nutrition and exer-cise, books that tell about labor and delivery. Understanding the changes your body is going through and what you can do for your and the baby's well-being is very important. But that's not all that needs tending during these nine months. Being pregnant is also an emotional and spiritual journey, a preparation of heart and soul.

Blessed Expectations is about that preparation, about the spiritual and emotional thrills and chills you'll experience on the way to giving birth. It's not about your body; it's about your soul. It's about your spiritual expansion, your emotional development, and your readiness to become a mother. It's about the sacrifices, the lessons, the intangibles. It's about the joy of anticipation, dreaming about who this baby will be. It's about waiting, reflecting, and partaking in surprise blessings along the way. It's about forgiveness and living fully. It's about experiencing the wonder of it all and not missing a moment of one of the most magnificent and transformational happenings of your life. *Blessed Expectations* is about your birth as a mother.

When I worked as a social worker in the emergency room of a large hospital, one of my duties was to cover labor, delivery, and obstetrics. I provided counseling and referral—a listening ear as it were—to new mothers, fathers, friends, and extended family. Whenever I went to the obstetrics unit, I was immediately reminded of the emotional and spiritual nature of childbirth. Many women were not prepared for the magnitude of their experience and were emotionally overwhelmed. The nature of a hospital is hustle and bustle, and, in this atmosphere, the need of the new family simply to be quiet—in order to get their bearings—frequently gets lost in the shuffle. Even before the baby arrives, it's easy to lose sight of the miracle you are participating in. But if you do, you risk losing out on the joys of pregnancy. *Blessed Expectations* is full of meditations and prayers to guide you on your path as you ready yourself for motherhood and prepare to welcome a little one into your family. Let it lead you through your nine-month journey with grace, joy, and laughter. From morning sickness, stretch marks, food cravings, and decorating the nursery, and from pregnant sex, your spouse, and the baby blues, you'll learn to sift through the troublesome glitches to discover satisfaction and delight in your pregnancy. When you're moody and can't touch your toes, when you're exhausted, fearful, and want this baby out, *Blessed Expectations* will help you remember what the journey's all about.

It's been almost nineteen years since my daughter Amanda was born, yet her arrival is fresh in my mind. Memories of morning sickness, exhaustion, and a difficult delivery fade quickly as I remember hearing her heart beat and seeing her cloudy image on the ultrasound. The day I felt her move, I no longer minded the discomfort; I was falling in love, and her kick stirred in me a new determination to not only be the best mother I could be, but the best person. I wanted her to have the very best start in life, and, while there were forces beyond my control, I did have power over my words, actions, and attitudes. My pregnancy, with all its contradictions, taught me to let go, surrender, and accept, so I could be a mother.

For all of us, pregnancy is the beginning of the quest to know yourself enough so that when your baby arrives you'll be able to do whatever is needed to parent your child. The changes you'll be going through may at times be overwhelming. When you need encouragement along the way, let this book be your pregnancy coach, urging you to take time to connect with the blessings. You can read *Blessed Expectations* in spurts or all the way through. Some topics will be more relevant early on; others will take on significance as your due date gets closer. Look at the table of contents and be guided by your intuition as to which sections to read when. As you find a section, a page, or sentence that speaks to you right then, mark it so you can reread it and share it with your husband. In doing so you'll transform your waiting into reflection and reap the many rewards that pregnancy itself can offer.

From the moment you learned you were pregnant, you entered a new phase of your life, opening your heart to greater dimensions of love. The stories in this book are here to cheer you on through the maze of feelings, thoughts, fears, and joys you'll experience as you discover within you a divine depth of love for yourself, your spouse, and this fresh unborn soul. Regardless of whether your pregnancy was planned or a surprise, even if your circumstances are less than perfect, you can begin now to lay the groundwork for greeting your baby with a welcome suitable for a child of God.

As you begin this book, I share with you the insight of my friend, a wise and juicy grandmother, "Pregnancy and childbirth are the highest of spiritual experiences. I only wished I would have known at the time."

And so as the preparations begin, let the blessings unfold.

Sweet Anticipation

Sweet Anticipation is dipping the stick, holding your breath, and looking closely again before showing your husband. It's lying still for the ultrasound, searching for the nebulous profile of your baby and asking, "Is everything okay?" It's a sigh of relief when you're told that it is.

It's the excitement of announcing the news and seeing the look on your mother's face when you tell her she's going to be a grandmother. It's the prospect of giving life that came from your love. It's imagining who this little person inside you will be. Will she look like you? Will he have his dad's eyes? What is her soul's purpose?

Sweet Anticipation is touching your belly, enchanted with tiny hiccups and kicking. It's suffering with nausea, heartburn, and gas. It's wasting days reading lists of names, double-checking and making sure none are forgotten. It's picking out colors for the nursery, buying a crib and a rocking chair. It's swooning as you fold each terry sleeper. It's crying over sappy TV commercials and counting the days.

Count Your Blessings

nnie and Rick were married in an English-looking chapel in the countryside not far from Seattle. Just prior to the ceremony, the minister asked if they would like a blessing for children included. Annie nodded yes and gave her soon-to-be husband a questioning look. Rick sheepishly nodded affirmatively and the short blessing was added: "And, when it is God's will for the procreation of children and their nurture in the knowledge and love of the Lord, bestow on them, if it is your will, the gift and heritage of children, and the grace to bring them up to know you, to love you, and to serve you."

Two weeks later, Annie had a spurt of energy. "I got up at the crack of dawn, picked buckets of blackberries, went home, made jam, then slept for seventeen hours. Three weeks after the wedding, I took an early pregnancy test and sure enough, just as I suspected, I was pregnant."

Marriage, pregnancy, and childbirth are indeed blessings with profound obligations. If you've ever held a cooing baby in your arms, you know the blessing of an innocent, smiling baby. But not everyone knows the blessings of pregnancy and childbirth. Those special blessings are known only to women, particularly women in the last half of this century, as birth control became available. Unlike women in generations before us or women in third world countries, we can, with comparative ease, plan how many children we want and regulate the timing of them. We're fortunate to be able to make choices about having children based on personal preference; our grandmothers and great-grandmothers, who often had six to ten pregnancies, were at the mercy of their fertility. You, on the other hand, have a wide array of choices and the good fortune to have an abundance of information at your fingertips and modern medicine to assist in ways you choose. Those are just the beginning of the advantages you can partake of.

Having a baby at the end of the nine-month journey is miraculous of course, but sprinkled along the way is ample good fortune, and, if you are willing to look past the side effects, you'll surely find the windfall. You're participating in the grandest of missions—in partnership with the Almighty, you are creating life. You are part of the divine process for the continuation of life. When you think of your pregnancy in this way, you realize what a precious gift has been bestowed upon you.

Pregnancy is a wonderland of mystery. From the fertilization of an egg with a sperm comes the genetic makeup to form a one-of-a-kind human being. Sex and eye color are determined from the start, and, before you ever feel anything, your body is making all kinds of precise adjustments to house the tiny cargo. By eight weeks the embryo has fingers and toes, hair and ears.

Pregnancy moves you from one stage of your life to another—from being a wife and career woman to also being someone's mother. It gives your life new purpose, adds richness and texture to it. So much is happening so quickly, from hearing the swish of a heartbeat, getting a black and white glimpse on the ultrasound, to being kicked in the ribs; there's never a dull moment.

Despite all its aches and pains, pregnancy brings evidence of the Divine's functioning in our human existence. If you pay close attention to what is going on within you, you won't be bored when you're expecting. Start by noticing your thoughts and feelings—perhaps keep a journal in which you record the changes in your body and what emotions those changes stir within you. As you open to your thoughts and feelings, you will gain a deeper understanding of yourself—that in itself is a blessing. And as you make the inquires into your own emotions, thoughts, hopes, dreams, and fears, you garner the strength and skill to muster the effort that pregnancy and childbirth require of you.

CELEBRATE THE GOOD NEWS

fter two years of fertility treatments, Margo and Sam had given up on having a baby, so when Margo learned she was expecting, she was stunned. She left the doctor's office, walked across the street to a pay phone, and called her husband. "Don't ask questions, just meet me as soon as you can at the sandwich shop," she said. "I'll be waiting for you." Hanging up, she immediately headed for a toy store, bought the biggest teddy bear she could find, tied blue and pink ribbons around it, plopped it in the chair across from her, and waited for her husband. Passersby gave her knowing glances, but she didn't mind; her heart was singing lullabies.

Sam couldn't break away from work for over an hour; he couldn't concentrate and wondered what his wife was up to. The first thing he spotted when he finally walked into the restaurant was the teddy bear, and, as he joined Margo at her table, he was careful not to let her see how annoyed and embarrassed he felt. "What's up?"

"I've started a teddy bear collection," she replied.

"Is that what you called me down here for?"

"I wanted to know if you'd help me pick one out each month until our baby gets here."

"What are you talking about?"

"I'm buying teddy bears for our baby!"

When he caught his breath, he took her hand, exclaiming, "Let's get out of here." They sat in their car hugging, laughing, and crying, while Sam kept asking, "Are you sure?" When Margo convinced him that it was true, he took her back to the toy store and he bought the second teddy bear—then they went to her parents to announce the news.

Be sure to celebrate your pregnancy. By celebrating, you're recognizing a major life experience, and you're affirming the joy that accompanies the news. Whether you decide to announce your pregnancy over a festive dinner with relatives or choose first to celebrate quietly with your husband, place your emphasis on what it means to you to be part of a family. At the end of nine months, you'll have a new little family member, so this is an appropriate time to talk about what family means to you. When you celebrate with your husband, friends, and family, you're not only sharing your happiness, you're including them in the process. You're inviting them to give you support and courage as you begin to ready yourself to give birth and to parent this child. As a mother to be, you need an abundant supply of support and nurturing from others so that you will be filled with love and able to pour that love into your baby. Offer a simple prayer of affirmation: I am thankful for life growing inside my body, for my husband, my family, and my friends.

Every couple needs to celebrate in their own way. Don't feel you have to immediately tell the whole world, if that doesn't feel right. Toni and Brad waited twelve years to have a baby and were cautious about celebrating too soon. It wasn't until the ultrasound at sixteen weeks assured them of a healthy boy that Toni could relax and live it up with a gourmet lunch including Grandma-to-be Patricia.

Commemorate your pregnancy any way you wish. Shout it from the treetops, call your friends, send letters, hang a banner from your door. Alec and Crystal planned their pregnancy, but, when the doctor confirmed it was twins, they walked around in a daze until they'd adjusted—then they called everyone they knew. Crystal said, "I couldn't stop smiling," Alec said, "I was so proud, I wanted everyone to know."

This is your special happening, and whether this is your first, second, or fourth baby, it's natural to share the excitement. Declare the good news, savor every moment, and you'll feel positively alive.

Vow to Treat Yourself Gently

hether you're a few weeks' pregnant or in your ninth month, make a promise to treat yourself kindly, compassionately, and with tender, loving care. Whenever you feel less than glorious, give yourself a gentle word instead of berating yourself. Stop comparing yourself to others or to the imaginary perfect mother-to-be in your head. Your pregnancy is unique, and, although you may have heard of a woman in her eighth month running a ten-kilometer race, or of someone in her seventh month who still looks cute in a swimming suit, remind yourself that the continuum of experiences is vast. Some of your experiences will be similar to your friends', others very different. Comparing your pregnancy and your feelings to other women's will only lead to discouragement. Remind yourself that your unique experience is exactly right for you to grow into a loving mother. As you're gentle with yourself, your baby will absorb your kindhearted ways.

What does it mean to treat yourself gently as a mother-to-be? It means recognizing that from the moment of conception your body is in a state of flux. It is going through tremendous physical changes, and you're likely to feel out of balance as you adjust. In the first weeks of your pregnancy, your body is preparing to function as an incredible life support system for your baby, and, in the final weeks, your body shifts again as it prepares for birth. There are the noticeable changes everyone can see as your tummy protrudes and you wear maternity clothing. Then there are the subtle fluctuations no one except you notices—your skin's itching and flaking, your underlying fears of labor pains, and your doubts about your ability to handle all the challenges. Treating yourself gently means that you take it easy on yourself, and, even if you don't know exactly what that means, you agree to experiment until you find what gives you comfort.

If you need to go to sleep every night at seven o'clock, go ahead. Try not to lay a guilt trip on yourself because you're feeling anxious or moody. Pregnancy brings with it out-of-control feelings; you're bound to feel afraid or apprehensive. Fear is normal, so be gentle with your fears by going slowly and not blaming yourself for feeling anxious. Be merciful to yourself. The needs of your unborn child are intimately connected to your taking good care of yourself physically, emotionally, and spiritually. Harshness and self-criticism have no place in your pregnancy, and as you learn to show tenderness toward yourself you'll be able to show compassion for the confusion and fear your partner or other children may be experiencing. Caring for the people you love—including your unborn child—begins by kindly caring for yourself.

> *My child looked at me and I looked back at him in the delivery room,*
> *and I realized that out of a sea of infinite possibilities it had come down to*
> *this: a specific person, born on the hottest day of the year, conceived on a*
> *Christmas Eve, made by his father and me miraculously from scratch.*

—Anna Quindlen

Put Yourself Front and Center

nnie took an early pregnancy test, but she didn't tell Rick that blue meant yes. She kept it to herself and mulled it over privately, "I'm sorry for this early deception, but this pregnancy had to be mine for awhile," she said later to Rick. "I needed time to sort things out and absorb how being pregnant would affect my life. I wanted to handle the business details of my life, how my pregnancy would affect my schooling, my end of our finances. I wanted to think about it alone first." Annie was taking care of herself first, which is an important consideration for every pregnant woman.

Putting yourself front and center means treating yourself with consideration and taking into account your special needs first and foremost. What do you, the mother-to-be, need in order to be content and at ease? Right now that is what matters most. Bette, for example, got heartburn whenever she ate a full meal, and, even though dinner was a special time for her and her husband, she felt better when she ate frequent protein snacks throughout the day. She explained to Adam that although she wouldn't be eating big dinners she didn't expect him to change his routine for her. He said, "I'm glad you're taking care of yourself, because, when you do, you're taking good care of our baby."

You might be like Abbey, whose morning sickness lasted all day, or Sally, who says, "My morning sickness comes around two-thirty, so I keep a large supply of rice cakes and saltines in my desk at work, because, when I feel dizzy, I need crackers right away." Think of all the ways you can make yourself more comfortable. At work, Jessica put a stool under her desk so she could put her feet up, and at lunchtime she took a snooze on a blanket in a nearby park. Remember that pregnancy can be disorienting. Moms-to-be say as their body changes, the center of gravity shifts and they're clumsy, "I bump into things, break dishes, and spill on myself every time I eat." Pregnant life is topsy-turvy. Things that were once appealing often take a back burner. By her third month, Colleen, an artist known for her abstract nudes, couldn't pick up a brush without painting a baby. Maggie, a computer analyst, surprised herself when all she wanted to do was shop for yarn and knit baby sweaters.

Pregnancy is all consuming. Your thoughts and energy are on babies, families, and the changes in your body, so don't expect yourself to concentrate on the newspaper, the stock market, or politics. World events are boring in comparison to bringing in new life. That's okay. Don't deny yourself the perks of being pregnant. Your hormones are out of whack, so you're entitled to change your mind. Just because you signed up for the mommy's exercise class doesn't mean you have to show up everyday. You can play hooky without guilt. The other moms will envy you, wonder where you got so much courage.

Putting yourself front and center means listening to what your body and soul need and want. If you don't feel like jumping out of bed with morning sickness to do a load of laundry before going to you work, indulge yourself. You don't have to do it all. You will survive, even if the beds don't get made or the house doesn't look immaculate.

> *Babies are bits of star-dust blown from the hand of God. Lucky the woman who knows the pangs of birth for she has held a star.*
>
> —Larry Barretto

Sit Down When You're Tired

f this is your first pregnancy, you might be surprised at how tired you are, especially in the first months. Marne said, "Right away I suspected I might be pregnant because I was so tired, but until I knew for sure I wondered if I had chronic fatigue syndrome."

Your body is literally supporting the lives of two, and as you adjust you can expect to be tired. Exhaustion and fatigue not only plague the first trimester, but continue off and on until your baby is on a regular sleeping schedule. Initially, your body is working harder than it ever has to be the life-support system for your baby, and, following the birth, your body is adjusting to a nonpregnant state while you are caring for a new-born, who sleeps in small increments.

Being tired is a signal from your body that you need to take a rest. Sitting and staring into space doesn't mean you're lazy, it means you're listening and responding to the messages from your body. Taking good care of your body when it's worn out is taking good care of your baby. When you feel exhausted, don't push yourself a minute longer! Instead, give yourself a thirty-minute BBB—baby-body-break. If it is hard for you to indulge yourself, think of it this way: The time you devote to refreshing yourself now is good training for after the baby comes—by then you'll need to be an experienced catnapper.

Give yourself a BBB several times each day. Taking thirty-minute naps when you notice that you're beginning to feel weary will help you bounce back quicker than if you wait until you're dragging. Some mornings you may feel so fatigued that you'll sleep in later. Remind yourself that it's really okay to stay in bed and read. Mimi said she found stretching more invigorating than napping so she gave herself a chance to stretch morning, afternoon, and evening.

When fatigue creeps upon you and threatens your energy, it's time to let others know that you're physically and emotionally spent. Some days you'll have no energy for the household tasks, errands, or entertaining, so let your husband, mother, or friends pitch in, especially when they offer or ask how they can help. Don't be shy in letting them know what would be helpful. Kelsey mentioned to her mother-in-law that she felt queasy at the smell of food, and that it was worse in the evening when she tried to cook dinner. When her mother-in-law offered to stock the freezer with easy-to-warm-up meals, Kelsey surprised herself by saying, "That would be wonderful."

As your pregnancy progresses, remember that when your back aches, your feet are swollen, or your rings no longer slip past your knuckle, it's a good idea to sit down and put your feet up as often as you can. As you rest your body, notice how your thoughts have been racing with all the things you need to get done. Let your thoughts come and go without getting absorbed in them. As you allow your mind to slow down, your body will relax. Notice the points of tension in your body. Relax each muscle group, your feet and legs, your thighs, your belly and back, your arms and shoulders, your neck, face, and head. As the tension in your body dissolves, continue to empty your mind of thoughts and soak up the peace of this baby-body-break. By letting yourself sit down when you're tired you'll soon acquire a tranquil aura about you that will give a sense of well-being to your family.

Let us make pregnancy an occasion when we appreciate our female bodies.

—Merete Leonhardt-Lupa

Invest in a Name Book

he first purchase *Lauren made after the stick turned blue* on the home pregnancy test was a baby-naming book. It became her nightly reading material. She and Michael took turns pronouncing the names out loud: Aaron, Amos, Barnaby, Ashley, Beatrice, Charlene, Dottie. If they couldn't pronounce the name or decipher which gender it designated, or if it brought gales of laughter, they crossed it off the list. Finally, they narrowed the choices to two boys' names and two girls' names. Then they shared the names with friends and family, "A huge mistake," Lauren said, "because everyone gave us an opinion or offered a name they thought was better." Since everyone you know will have opinions as to the best name, more and more couples are keeping it a secret. Joe and Alexia bought a name book and perused for names that fit their criteria. They wanted a name that sounded good with their last name, that was original but not cutesy, up-to-date but not too trendy. Over the next few months, without consulting family or friends, they narrowed the selection to one boy's and one girl's name and kept the names a secret. When anyone asked, they politely said, "We're not telling yet." Once the baby was born, they revealed their choice to the world. Since it was a done deal, no one could complain.

The quest to find just the right name for your little bundle of joy is fun, but you'll probably have to sharpen your negotiation skills; after all, agreeing on your baby's name is the first of many joint parenting decisions—no fair deciding this one on your own. Start the name game early, because you're likely to be navigating and negotiating your way through fads and family traditions. It took Rodney and Jane eight and a half months to agree to break a tradition of naming the baby after a great grandparent. They mulled it over, had heated conversations, and listed the pros and cons before they both were comfortable with an original, up-to-date name. The Hornes wanted an old-fashioned name. The Allens focused on finding a name with an acceptable nickname, the Siegels let their eight-year-old daughter pick the final name from three that they'd selected. Andrea and Colleen bought a name book that gave the meaning and origin of names: "We wanted to know the significance before we decided." The birth announcement gave the baby's name and the name's meaning: Eleanor, a light or bright torch.

Perhaps you'd like to give your baby a name with a meaning to reflect who you sense she or he is. To do that, choose, in concert with your husband, several names you think might reflect your child's inner light. Hold the names privately, where they will rest in your heart for seven days. Come together and say each name out loud, making the final choice in accordance with your hearts. On a specially chosen piece of paper, perhaps parchment or linen, write a greeting: We give you the name _____, which means _____. Sign your names and the date. Roll the paper and tie it with a ribbon. Put it with the special mementos you're saving to give your child one day.

Many parents advise taking a list of possible names to the hospital because you might not know for sure if the name you've chosen is exactly right until you're acquainted with your baby. You may like the name Shay, but your little girl may actually look more like a Susannah, and while Harry may be your number one choice for a boy, your son's energy and personality might be more like a Daniel's.

The first question friends and relatives ask is: "Is it a boy or girl?" followed by "What's the baby's name?" With so many names, so many options, and only nine months to decide, start thinking about it soon. This is the fun part, so be sure to enjoy it to the fullest.

> *Birth is the sudden opening of a window through which you look out upon*
> *a stupendous prospect.*
>
> —William Dixon

Rise Above the Physical Glitches

here's physical discomfort in pregnancy. Michele, forty-two years old and thrilled to be expecting her first child, describes it best, "I've got a lot of aches and pains with my pregnancy, so I've been figuring out how to get smoothly through the physical glitches." Michele's back goes out so often that she has scheduled weekly appointments with a chiropractor. She's discovered that her best back aid is tucking a white boat bumper behind her tail bone for support. In her thirty-seventh week, she scoots the cumbersome bumper behind her each time she sits down. Shifting to get comfortable, Michele points out, "Regardless of all the physical discomfort, I've never resented the baby. The baby is totally exempt—that's just the way it is." She smiles as she thinks out loud, "I wonder if that will continue when he's smearing peanut butter on my new drapes?"

What a miracle pregnancy brings! With each physical annoyance comes an opportunity for the transformation of your spirit. Often when someone hurts you or causes you pain or trouble, you're apt to feel perturbed, resentful, hostile, or mean. You might try to avoid that person, strike back, or get even. But now that you're expecting, most likely your attitude is different. You're able to see that your suffering has a purpose, and, even though your back aches continuously, your shoulders cramp so tightly you can barely move your neck, and charley horses grip your legs in the middle of your deepest sleep, you're able to rise above your impulses to get even. You're able to ignore the urge to run away, and you willingly endure this temporary misery for the sake of having your child.

My friend Cheri had a complicated pregnancy and was ordered to stay in bed for months. Inconvenient and boring, it certainly wasn't how she'd planned to spend her final months. At times she was down in the dumps and depressed—but she never wavered in her dedication to the well-being of her unborn child. Her husband, Ron, washed her hair as she dangled her head over a basin at the side of the bed. She entertained friends, paid bills, folded the clothes, and calculated the year-end taxes all from bed. With all the physical challenges of her pregnancy, she never gave up and she never blamed her baby.

Cheri certainly didn't want to stay in bed but she wanted a baby, so she prayed to find the blessing in her circumstance. Sometimes she was so eager for the time to pass that she felt she was jumping out of her skin, so she prayed longer and asked her friends to pray, too. She was helpless to change her situation, so she looked to find something positive. She read old books and magazines she'd been saving. She called old friends and renewed connections. She really listened to music. She wrote letters in longhand and poured out her heart. She completed the afghan she'd started knitting three years earlier. She found satisfaction in seeing her project completed.

Perhaps it's through the pangs of discomfort that the insignificant fades and we learn to rise above setbacks and disappointments to find what truly matters in our lives. If gold doesn't pass through fire it remains impure; in passing through fire it's stripped of impurities and polished to its highest radiance. So perhaps the pains and discomfort of pregnancy and childbirth are the Almighty's way of polishing our souls for the passage into motherhood.

When you are feeling particularly challenged in your pregnancy, remind yourself that this is a preparation for parenting. With the wisdom you've gained, you will be better able to embrace the challenges of parenting rather than shrink from them.

When I had almost reached term, I looked like a rat dragging a stolen egg.

—Colette

CHERISH YOUR BABY'S FATHER

ince pregnancy is an all-consuming endeavor, you might get so absorbed in what's going on inside of you that you don't notice what's going on for your husband. But you're both becoming parents, and as he becomes familiar with his new identity, he'll have his own highs and lows. Adding a new member to the family is a giant emotional and financial commitment, and, although your husband made the choice to be a father, he might be overwhelmed by his impending obligations. Fathers-to-be are bound to be out-of-sorts and preoccupied with how their lives are changing. If you can put yourself in your husband's shoes and see things from his perspective, you'll avoid bruised feelings and cold shoulders. Besides you'll be more able to get excited together!

Your baby's father-to-be is probably having a wide range of doubts, from, "This is way too expensive for me," and "I didn't know she'd act like this," to "Will we ever have fun again?" "Will I be a good father?" and "Is the baby okay?" Studies have found that many expectant fathers actually experience sympathetic pregnancy symptoms. This is called couvade syndrome (a French word for "to hatch"). Some men have gained weight and had food cravings, leg cramps, and sporadic labor pains. No one knows for sure why this happens, but there's speculation that it may have to do with feeling guilty about causing discomfort for their wives. Or it may be a way of trying to share in the experience. Nick and Rosalie are very much in tune with one another, so it isn't surprising that Nick felt as though he was expecting, too. In the third month, Rosalie stopped throwing up, but Nick began having bouts of nausea, and, as Rosalie had energy spurts, Nick was exhausted.

Not all husbands experience such symptoms, but they are experiencing many feelings. Nicole was very honest when she told me, "It's a challenge to give attention to my husband, because all my focus is on my baby. Bill knows he's taken second place and doesn't know what to do about his feelings of jealousy." Although you might not feel the same as Nicole, it's easy to understand that your husband may feel pushed away as you focus on your pregnancy, and again when you're consumed with baby care. Reassure him that you appreciate him. Take time to ask him about his day. Tell him you know it's a challenging adjustment. Ask him how he's feeling now that he's sharing you. If he says misses your attention, respond by listening, and ask him for suggestions. Just knowing that you are sensitive to his position will make it easier for both of you.

Some men are unconsciously jealous because their wives get all the attention, credit, and glory while they take the backseat. Others resent not being her "little boy" anymore. The reasons why he feels the way he does don't matter as much as how you respond. Arguing or disapproving of his thoughts will not solve the problem. Even if you don't comprehend what he's going through, try to understand. You may not need to say anything. Simply listening for the meaning and feelings underneath the words can be enough, especially when you respond with an affirmative nod and a smile.

If he seems to take the news of your pregnancy in stride, don't be too disappointed. He might need adjustment time. Don't be jealous if he needs some time alone to go fishing, work on his car, or play golf with his buddies. Don't assume he knows how much you still love him—be sure to tell him. You know you need your husband, but sometimes it's easy to forget that your husband also needs you! Although he may be bigger and stronger, he needs you to understand that he has fears, too, and occasionally needs reassurance and comfort from you.

Thank him for participating with you. Surprise him with a thank-you and toast him with sparkling water when he puts together the crib or rubs your back. Give your husband his first daddy gift and let him know how glad you are to have him in your life and how happy you are that he's the father of your child.

$\mathcal{I}$NCREASE ISLANDS OF TOGETHERNESS

or reasons that can't be adequately explained, expecting a baby is a very sentimental thing, perhaps because it's not a singular event but rather a joint undertaking. You and the man you love have embarked on a nine-month journey that gives you a chance to know each other in a deeper way. You're interdependent now, and a synchronicity is arising between the two of you and your unborn child.

When Marla was about one month pregnant, she packed a big picnic and took Jake to the park. Jake was already the father of two children from a previous marriage, and, although they had frequently talked about having children together, she wanted to talk it over one more time before she shared her suspicion. "Would you like to have more children?" she asked. His response melted her heart. "I've prayed that God would give me a third chance." He acknowledged that he hadn't been there when his two children were babies and wanted the chance to be a better father to an infant and a better husband for his wife. For that afternoon, that bench became an island where she listened to Jake's anguish at not being there for his first wife and their sons. Difficult though it was to hear his pain, she listened as he poured out his heart. Her listening was a healing force, and provided the impetus, too, for him to face his responsibilities and take steps to make things right.

An island of togetherness is full of possibilities for healing, for closeness, for understanding, for romance—especially romance, because amid all the baby preparation, sometimes the romance and the love between the two of you gets forgotten. But it doesn't have to be that way. Expanding your family can have a romantic aspect, especially when you're willing to talk to each other like you did when you were courting. You have new experiences to share. Ask your partner how his life has changed since your pregnancy. Tell him what you're looking forward to. Listen carefully to each other. You'll renew your relationship as you share the events of the day. You may not be able to solve each other's problems, but you can be one another's sounding boards.

It's such a pleasure coming home at the end of the day to see the face of your beloved. Spending time together ignites some of the spark that brought you first together. Quality time doesn't need to be elaborate. The most tender moments are often the simplest: sitting on the step while your husband washes the car, reading the newspaper over breakfast, taking a walk. Sometimes you don't need words to feel the loving energy between you; other times you want to express what you're thinking and feeling.

Lauren said, "As my husband worked at his computer, I'd slip up quietly and put my hand on his back and kiss his cheek, or I'd sit beside him and read. Sometimes we wouldn't say a word, but he'd look over at me with such tenderness that for a brief moment we were on our own island of togetherness."

Snuggling, hugging, holding hands, laughing, smiling, and listening will transport you to your own island—you can go there for brief intervals several times each day. Healing moments of togetherness are the invisible glue that holds a couple and a family together. They are the reason you came together in the first place.

> *To the mother alone it has been given, that her soul during the nine months should touch the soul of the child.*
>
> —Jean Baptiste Lacordaire

Treasure Your Baby's Movements

t first you might not recognize the rolling sensations, twitches, and tingles in your belly as the movements of your baby, but at around twenty-two weeks, your little one, who weighs slightly over a pound, can kick so vigorously that you'll begin to take bets on whether he's a soccer player or a ballet dancer. Your baby is having a rollicking good time jumping, rolling, and pushing you around and may surprise you by responding to your touch with a wiggle. She might have the hiccups—they feel like tiny thumps—and jump or jerk at loud noises. You're in touch with your baby, and his blows are reassuring.

By the time you can detect your baby's movements, a lot of development has taken place. In the first trimester there was an explosion of cell activity. The reproductive cells called gametes have become a fertilized egg called a zygote, which divides to become a mass of cells known as morula, which turn into fluid-filled cells called a blastocyst, which then becomes the embryo. At the five-week mark, you're hooked up through the placenta and umbilical cord to the developing embryo, which by twelve weeks is a two-and-a-half-inch-long fetus with fingers, toes, and ears. That's why you were seasick and worn out!

By fourteen weeks, as you come out of your Sleeping Beauty coma and begin to look like a mother-to-be, you delight in the glow of pregnancy. Your hair and middle are thicker and your breasts are overflowing. You're in good spirits with energy to shop for maternity clothes and baby books. By the end of twenty-eight weeks your baby's lungs have developed to a point where survival outside the womb is possible; he weighs two and a half pounds and is ten inches long.

By the eighth month, you're thankful to be in the home stretch—your bladder is squished, you're plagued with heartburn, and your swaybacked gait is noticeable. Your baby is in a flurry of activity, opening and shutting her eyes, poking you with her elbows, and sometimes sucking her thumb. At week thirty-six, you've attended childbirth classes, packed your bag, and studied the quickest route to the hospital. By the thirty-ninth week, you're thinking about labor, you're short of breath, and you want this baby out! Your baby has dropped into position and your pregnant belly is lower. There's not much room left for wiggling, but your baby still moves about ten times each day. Every time your baby moves you'll automatically touch your belly, you're eager to meet each other and the message is clearly, "Won't be long now, see you soon."

Getting kicked by your unborn baby is a blessing in itself. When you feel it, tune in so you don't miss it. You knew that there was a baby growing in your body, but her kicking made it real. What a precious greeting! Cherish every tiny jiggle, every little ripple. Your baby might stretch so wide that you can actually see his foot or her hand bulging out your side. What could be more thrilling? Treasure all this motion; there's not another feeling like it!

> *It is only when the rigidity of advanced pregnancy sets in that you appreciate fully how useful it was to be able to bend at the waist.*
>
> —Audrey Hull

GET PRACTICAL

here are practical matters to take care of. You don't have to do them all at once, but here's a list to get you started.

1. Who is going to deliver your baby? A doctor or a midwife? You want to make this decision early because you want a compatible match. You may have an obstetrician in mind or know a friend who used a midwife. Use these recommendations to point you in the right direction. Make an appointment to meet in person to learn about her. Find someone who is willing to sit down—while you're still dressed—to answer your questions. Before you go for the interview, make a list of questions. What does he think about pain medication, natural childbirth, husbands as coaches, length of hospital stay? Ask who covers for your doctor if you go into labor when she's off duty. Bring your husband along. Don't be afraid to change your mind.

Alyce eliminated one doctor because he ignored her and talked directly to her husband. For her second baby, Stephanie decided against the doctor who had delivered her first child, because she hadn't been comfortable with the way the doctor explained her need for a cesarean. Decide on the doctor or midwife whose philosophy matches your own, and tell her or him what's important to you. Consider her bedside manner. You want professionals around you who are positive, encouraging, understanding, patient, and willing to give you the information you ask for. This is your baby, your delivery. By making your wishes known, you'll find a compatible match with a birthing team and avoid unnecessary disappointments.

2. Where are you going to have the baby? At home or in the hospital? If your city has several hospitals, you can choose your doctor from the list that practices in the hospital you choose. Call the hospital and make an appointment for a tour. Ask about their visiting policies and whether young children can be present.

3. If you have a boy, do you want a circumcision? If so, ask your doctor who does it, the obstetrician or pediatrician?

4. Choose a pediatrician. Call the office and ask if they are accepting new patients. Don't assume they automatically will. Maddy waited until the last minute and was disappointed when she learned that the pediatrician she wanted wasn't taking anyone new. If that happens, ask the doctor or assistant if they can recommend someone.

5. It's natural for you to have lots of questions, so don't be afraid to ask for clarification about anything you don't fully understand. Even if this is not your first pregnancy you can't possibly know all the answers. Everything from amniocentesis, constipation, morning sickness, shortness of breath, contractions, and membranes rupturing in public could be on your mind. To avoid forgetting anything, make a list in between office visits and be sure to bring it with you. It's helpful to bring along your husband so you can both remember what has been said. Chances are your head will be swimming.

6. Buy or borrow a set of progressive relaxation video- or audiotapes. Practice the exercises as much as you can. Rene said, "I thought the exercises couldn't possibly help. I was wrong. Just knowing I had those to fall back on gave me confidence not only during childbirth, but through amnio, the ultrasound, and whenever I felt anxious."

7. It's never too soon to start planning for help after the birth. It's better to err on the side of too much help, especially if this is your first baby. When Rick, forty-two, called to share the good news about his first child, he exclaimed, "It takes all three of us—me, my wife, and mother-in-law—just to get through the day. I don't know how women do it alone!" I reassured him that things would get easier, but in the meantime he was appreciating the help. Even if you can't imagine leaving your baby for a minute, things will come up, and having good help will be reassuring to you. Start collecting names of baby-sitters. On their first visit, have them work while you're still there. Seeing them with your baby will put you at ease.

ℰXPERIENCE THE WONDER OF WAITING

efore you were expecting, you probably didn't find virtue in waiting around for life to take its own course. Like most modern women, you probably have a take-charge attitude—on the go and in control of making things happen. Now, however, waiting consumes your life: You wait at the doctor's office, wait to show, wait to feel your baby move, wait for labor. Once you were impatient to keep on schedule; now waiting troubles you less, and each trimester is full of unexpected happiness. You feel fortunate to be expecting. Your waiting is filled with pure expectancy. Oh sure, in the final weeks, you think about jumping up and down or standing on your head to hurry things along, but by now you've learned that pregnant waiting has its own special beauty.

You're in the pregnant state of mind, which is a blessing in itself. In this hurry-up, fast paced world, it's easy to become so intent on reaching a goal that you forget that the journey has its own reward. It's often when you've reached your goal and look back that you understand the joy in waiting and wish you hadn't hurried the process by thinking only of the end result. Through your pregnant journey, much of which is waiting, you have a chance to discover the richness in living each moment.

Pregnant waiting has a benediction and innocence about it. You try to imagine your baby's face, but you have to wait to see the color of her hair and eyes. You can't figure out if his personality will be more like yours or his dad's, so you settle into a phase of eager anticipation. It's exciting to wait because you know that your waiting will bring you a surprise more glorious than your imagination can conjure up.

Pregnant waiting is not just a statement about your physical condition—it's also a reference to your spiritual state of being. Mindful waiting is an aspect of spiritual growth that prepares you for the holy experience of birth. Your waiting is not passive, as you pay close attention to what is happening to your body without pushing before it's time. Attentive waiting is needed so that when the time is right you can take an active part.

Out of pregnant waiting, gratitude arises. When you're pregnant, thinking about what you're wishing for fades, because you know that the greatest miracle is taking place within and—in a certain way—beyond you. There's nothing left to wish for, because what could be more glorious than experiencing the fullness of life enveloping you like a cozy baby blanket?

Waiting is immensely beautiful. It helps you quiet your mind and makes room in your heart for more heavenly blessings to come. Every mother-to-be has within her tremendous capacity for love for her partner, her children, and herself. Waiting helps your old persona melt away so the divine mother in you can bloom. In a pregnant state of mind, you become in tune with the spiritual aspects of caring for a soul as you open to a greater dimension of your love and capacity for caring. Pregnant waiting wraps you in the sweet awareness that life is good.

> *Childbirth is more admirable than conquest, more amazing than self-defense, and as courageous as either one.*
>
> —Gloria Steinem

PLAN A SIMPLE NURSERY

ecorating and arranging the nursery is much more than painting and buying a crib; it's a symbol of welcoming as you make room in your home for a new family member. I once read a story of an actress who searched the world for the perfect crib and chose a round one to be placed in the center of the room. She wanted to provide an open environment for her baby and was convinced the roundness gave her baby a feeling of contentment not found in a rectangular crib.

You may not want a round crib, but, if you're like most expectant moms, you have a sense of the ambiance you want for your baby's room and will go out of your way to make sure it's right. Since you want to create a nursery that feels good when you're in it, remember: The love you put into choosing something special is more important than an updated changing table or the world's most expensive bassinet. The chuckle that the mobile brings is more important than whether it's new or borrowed.

If this is your first baby, you probably won't heed the advice to keep the nursery preparations simple. But if you already have a child, you'll understand the advantages of simplicity. First timers want everything new: crib, stroller, walker, high chair. Experienced parents know the value of hand-me-downs and the purpose of buying later. "Our first baby spent very little time in her nursery, because she wanted to be near us. With our second baby we're postponing doing his room; for now we've put a bassinet next to us so that when he's fussy it's easy to pile him into our bed."

Whether you're preparing a whole room or a comfy corner next to your bed, you're sending a special greeting of your time and commitment. As you prepare the baby's space, you're making the first of many monetary commitments. Instead of driving yourself over the edge by searching for the latest designer baby stuff or going broke buying furniture you can't afford, consider placing the emphasis on giving your new arrival a personalized spot in your home. Also consider giving your baby a gift that's a reflection of you. At Lydia's baby shower, her friends made a collage of colorful pictures and wishes to hang on the wall. You can be sure that it will be her child's treasured heirloom. Adam took six months to make a cradle, and, when other family members borrow it for their newborns, he carves the name and birth weight of each baby on the side. Candice decorated shelves with books and toys from her own childhood.

Perhaps this is a good time to reflect on what you value in your family. It seems as if we all get caught in the trap of material possessions. We know it's a trap, but we can't seem to break away from it, and we pass the tendency on to our children by insisting that everything they have be top of the line. So many children have closets full of toys they haven't played with, drawers full of clothes they haven't worn. When you prepare a simple nursery, you bring a reverence into your everyday life by thinking over each purchase carefully. Is a new crib what you want, or will a borrowed one from your sister be satisfactory, perhaps even more meaningful?

A simple nursery doesn't mean your baby has to go without; it simply means making a conscious choice of what you bring into your home. If you create your baby's nursery mindfully, you are on the way to living mindfully with your child. Simplicity sometimes means more: more time to rock your baby, more time to laugh. A cozy little corner full of positive love energy is more reassuring than pricey decorations.

Babies are such a nice way to start people.

—Don Herold

Go Swimming

xpecting is physically and emotionally depleting, and, even though you're delighted with your impending motherhood, there will be those unwieldy moments when you plot how to run away from it all. You're filled with doubts but you don't want to admit it. You're in an ornery mood, and, if one other person asks what's wrong, you'll scream. You don't want to take your frustrations out on the people you love, so before you snap or say something you regret, get yourself out of the house and locate the nearest swimming pool. You need a water cure. When out of the blue, a wave of sadness is upon you, you're anxious, fidgety, or on the verge of going over the edge; when you can't concentrate, you're restless, or you can't settle down—that's when you know it's time to get in water.

"Swimming is wonderful," notes Janie. "When I'm in the water I feel light, free, and non-pregnant. I can move and breathe, I feel like myself again." Swimming is more than physically rehabilitating; swimming puts you in touch with the basic element of life. For centuries, water has been the symbol of life, for all life depends on its purifying, cleansing, and replenishing. Before you jump into the water, close your eyes, stretch your arms over your head with palms open and slowly repeat three times: "With this water, let my heartaches and sorrows wash away." If you can't get to a swimming pool, stand at the sink, cup your hands, and let water flow over them. Or repeat this phrase while bathing or taking a shower.

Water, like life, is always moving. You can't feel stagnant when you're in it. You can't get stuck in a swimming pool; indeed you'll get physically and emotionally buoyed up, which is exactly what you need after carrying around an extra thirty-five or more pounds. Your baby is peacefully floating in the warmth of the amniotic sac, and you'll find that floating in warm water will soothe your nervous system, too. After thirty minutes of splashing, you'll unwind, burn off excess energy, and be back to your optimistic self. Even if you don't have the luxury of a swimming pool in your backyard and it's dead winter, you can always find a pool. There's a YMCA in almost every town, and many even have water aerobics classes for mothers-to-be.

Although swimming might entice you, the thought of putting on a swimming suit with your pregnant belly bulging might be terrifying. But compared to all those pelvic exams, how bad can it really be? If you're by the beach, don't deny yourself the ocean breezes just because of vanity. When you find yourself comparing your seven months' pregnant body to the bodies of teenage girls in bikinis and lamenting that you've lost your figure, remember this is how a mom-to-be looks. Besides, once you jump in, you'll feel so good you'll forget how you look.

> *Children are the purpose of life. We were once children and someone took care of us. Now it is our turn to care.*
>
> —Cree elder

aving a baby is an ordinary event with extraordinary blessings. Millions of women have done it before you; it happens every day. Nevertheless, when it's you who is pregnant, when it's you who is nauseated, when it's you who sees your role in life changing, it's definitely earth-moving. Whether this is your first, third, or sixth pregnancy, this is an occasion worthy of the highest, finest, and most lofty of intentions.

Having a baby is a rite of passage. It's a physical, emotional, and spiritual journey that marks a turning point in your life. The ups and downs of pregnancy provide the lessons inviting you to grow up and be a loving parent. We've all heard stories of someone who had a baby for selfish reasons. They didn't feel love in their own lives and had the mistaken idea that a baby would ensure that they'd be loved. We've heard people talking about having children as an insurance policy for their old age. These are selfish reasons; you and your baby deserve better.

A baby comes into the world a fresh and innocent spirit. You're the one chosen to nurture, protect, and guide her through her childhood. You're entrusted to care for his soul. As you watch over him and keep him safe, you allow his spirit to be free. When you consider where these precious souls come from, you'll aspire to be the best person and the best parent you can be.

There's no better opportunity than parenting to put your spirituality into action. Some mothers-to-be have perfectionist tendencies; they think that doing everything just right is best for their families. They pour on the pressure, which quickly backfires, causing anxiety and tension. When you strive to be perfect, you miss knowing yourself and your baby at the soul level. Striving and pushing yourself is not the highest choice; remaining open to God's grace is more satisfying. Grace is subtle, like the fragrance of a flower. It gives a new context and significance to your life. When grace has arrived, compassion is found, and all will be as it should be.

What does the Almighty have in store for you and this precious little soul? When you think you know what's best, you force and manipulate. But when you turn every-thing—from the smallest to the largest struggle—over to the highest good, you make room for guidance from above. What are the lessons you are learning right now? When your body aches and you're impatient, stop for a moment and let God in on the strug-gle. Get your spiritual practice in good working order so, when the baby has colic and you're weary from walking the floor, you'll know where to turn. With grace protect-ing you daily, you know that God is near. In these fast paced, hurry-up days, that's a windfall worth receiving.

> *Every woman in the ninth month of pregnancy is bound to be struck by the thought that the gestation period in human beings is far too long.*
>
> —Audrey Hull

Sing Lullabies, Listen to Music, and Dance

You *know how when you're listening to a vibrant symphony* and suddenly it's silent, the noise in your mind stops? You're able to turn out the demands of your hectic schedule and tune in to yourself. Listening to music helps you unwind, calm down, rest, and then once again get energized. Music helps you be alert and awake, yet silent and peaceful. The same is true for your unborn child. And if you sing sweet lullabies before your baby is born, she'll distinguish your voice right away and feel comforted by the reassuring melodies once she enters the outside world.

At around fourteen weeks, your developing baby can hear your heartbeat, your voice, and music. Your baby is in motion and can wave his tiny arms and legs. Studies show that babies before and after birth respond to beautiful music. Good music is a fun and reassuring way to communicate with your child. Try some Mozart, Vivaldi, or Kenny G. Or sing yourself.

There's a natural urge within mothers to sing to their babies. For centuries, mothers have been making up songs to express their love. Singing to your baby is calming and encircles you both with joy and goodwill. A lullaby is simple and repetitive, so you can make it up as you go or hum your favorite. It's the feeling of love that matters, not the words or whether you keep perfect pitch. Just a simple tune, with simple words, sung in whispers to your baby, imparts a sense of security.

Swaying and dancing gently is as comforting as any rocking chair. In primitive times, cradles were developed so busy moms could rock their babies with their feet and keep their hands free for work. And while the busy mothers worked, they sang lullabies that offered hope and connection for mother and child.

People have a desire to sing while working, and, if you let yourself get over feeling self-conscious, you'll find everyone in the household will stop and listen. There are many folk lullabies and tender melodies to choose from. Familiarize yourself with some up-to-date lullabies. If you don't want to sing on your own, try humming to Linda Ronstadt's album, *Dedicated to the One I Love*. Your baby will recognize your voice, and after birth will respond with coos of her own.

Listening to steady drum music or beating a drum in time with your own heartbeat will put you in touch with the rhythm that your baby is hearing. Your heartbeat is the baby's first drum, the beat of the universe. That's why babies like to sleep on your chest—the beat, beat, beat of your heart is soothing. Everybody enjoys a drum beat. Try it with your husband, put his head next to your heart and notice how fast he falls asleep.

If you belong to a pregnant moms' exercise class, suggest, as one mother-to-be did, that each class end with stretching and singing to a tape of lullabies or drumbeats. Then use the same music during labor to reassure your baby. The music and beats will also help your husband, who will definitely need fortifying by then.

A baby is someone just the size of a hug.

—Anonymous

Indulge Your Cravings

ating what you crave is one of the fringe benefits of pregnancy. You get to eat more freely, as both you and others are more forgiving of binges and bizarre appetite. Indulging yourself is understandable because, after all, you're craving for two. But it's not as simple as popping a bonbon in your mouth or dining on your favorite entree.

During the first two months, you'll be singing an "Oh, what shall I eat" sonnet. You're suffering from a peculiar combination of nausea and starvation. When you're feeling queasy, the mention of your favorite food makes you turn green, yet there's a pit in your stomach that only the right food quenches. One minute you're throwing up, the next minute you're ravenous. One minute you can't swallow a spoonful of your favorite yogurt, the next minute you're devouring the leftovers. It's a challenge to find a treat that calms your queasy stomach and satisfies your hunger. Old standbys might not be your staples now. Graze lightly and follow your instincts.

Fortunately, sensitivity to tastes and smells doesn't last forever, because by the second trimester, you usually can eat anything and handle most smells, except cigarette smoke, which you know isn't good for you anyway. By the end of your pregnancy, you might prefer small, frequent meals, since your squashed stomach leaves you feeling full and bloated, and you might suffer from heartburn if you overeat or eat too late at night.

There are as many different food cravings as there are mothers-to-be. "I ate perfectly when I was pregnant," said Katy. "My cravings were for veggies, fruit, and occasionally beef. I had no desire for junk. Sweets made me sick." You might not have a sweet tooth, but you might crave unheard of combinations: peanut butter and pickles or banana-and-brown-sugar sandwiches. Whatever you eat, Jayne, a midwife, advises her moms to, "Wash it down with plenty of water."

In a quandary about what to eat—chocolate cake or veggies—consider the nutritional value of your cravings. Some foods make you smart; some foods make you happy. You'll find a study somewhere to justify almost anything you're eating. There are experts who say eating spicy foods triggers the release of endorphins, the body's painkilling agents. Chocolate is a mood booster and helps you feel better and stay alert. Garlic calms you down and improves memory. Eating carbohydrates influences cognitive performance and helps you feel less anxious. And the right dose of sugar keeps you sharp. Do remember that what you eat or don't eat does affect your developing baby. One study found that if you suffer from excessive morning sickness, your child will crave salty snacks as he grows up. Your doctor will probably advise you to work your cravings into a balanced healthy diet, for it is crucial that you get the right amounts of vitamins and minerals. "I've craved a banana split for twenty-seven weeks," says Sonya. "But I haven't given in; instead, I binge on sardines and kimchee."

Respond to your food cravings, because your body knows exactly what it needs. Do as your mother says, "Eat lots of fruits and vegetables," and you won't have to worry. If in doubt, talk it over with your doctor.

In every child who is born, under no matter what circumstances, and of no matter what parents, the potentiality of the human race is born again.

—James Agee

Arrange for the Birth Day

our delivery date is calculated as forty weeks from the first day of your last period, which means unless your baby is early, you'll be waiting 280 days, more or less. The birth day is a big event, and with advance planning you can personalize it with your special style. You can't pinpoint the exact day or time unless you've scheduled a cesarean, but you can make preparatory arrangements that assure a birth suited to you and your partner.

What kind of experience do you want—a private event with a birth coach or a family affair with guests? Do you want to walk around during labor or stay in bed? What about pain medication? What about a midwife, underwater birth, or home delivery? Which hospital do you prefer? Take a tour of a birthing center and pick the one that's right for you.

Who will be your labor coach? Rita knew she was having twins and chose two labor coaches, her husband and her best friend, Paula. "They helped each other support me." Having two people staying positive and advocating for you gives you the freedom to respond to your body. Will your doctor or hospital accommodate that?

What do you want to wear during labor? Would you like an oversized cotton shirt or a lightweight flowing birthing robe? Whatever you choose, be practical so the nurse can easily check how far you've dilated and monitor the baby's heartbeat. Find something comfortable and cool—labor heats you up and you'll be sweating. Some women choose to wear nothing at all because it's irritating to have something rubbing or touching their skin. You don't want to get stuck in some scratchy hospital gown, so pack your bag in advance—then you won't have to decide on the spur of the moment. You can always take it off.

Would you like music? Natalie took Enya, Elton John, and the Boston Symphony.

Check in advance so you can bring along a tape or CD player if it's not provided. Do you want pictures? Dylon had planned to videotape, but left home without his camera. Think about the kinds of things that help you feel comfortable—a certain pillow, fresh flowers, a fragrant face wipe—then add them to your suitcase.

Anna stuffed two large bottles of her favorite sparkling water in her overnight bag, because she knew from previous experience that as soon as the doctor gave the word that it was okay to drink fluids, she'd be thirsty and might not want to wait for an aide to bring something from the cafeteria.

After all your plans, be willing to let go and accept what happens. Labor, like life, has its own rhythms. Noelle had a two-day labor that ended in a cesarean, not what she'd planned. Bonnie had a three-hour labor—only four hard pushes and she was done. Every labor is different—that's what keeps it interesting and new mothers talking. Think of it this way: When you take a wonderful vacation, you pick the spot, study the map, make the reservations, and look forward to what happens. The adventure comes, however, when you get off the main highway and travel an uncharted back road. In labor, as in the rest of nature, there are no fixed plans.

A baby is a well-spring of pleasure.

—Martin Tupper

PLAN A BLESSING AND BUY CIGARS

A *baby's arrival is a social event. Seventy-five years ago,* birth was still taking place at home or in the kitchen with family and friends assisting. Now, even though your birth will more than likely be in a hospital or birthing center with hired help, your friends, relatives, neighbors, and coworkers still will want to be included. They will be eager to know the details—what time was the baby born, the sex, the weight, does she have hair, and how are mom and dad? They'll want to celebrate with you. With a little advance preparation, you can make this an occasion to remember. It doesn't matter what you do, it can be simple or elaborate, as long as you emphasize how glad you are to have the support of family and friends.

If you want to send baby announcements, you might want to do as an organized friend of mine did. Address the envelopes while you're waiting, so that after the baby is here, all that's needed is to add the pertinent information. The same friend took a list of phone numbers with her to the hospital, because she knew she'd want to talk with friends as soon as the baby arrived.

Send your husband out to buy the cigars so he can participate in that manly rite of passage. The connection between smoke and babies dates back thousands of years. The ancient Mayans blew smoke to the heavens to delight the powers that be and to signal that the baby had arrived safely. American Indians passed the pipe when a father was blessed with a child. By sharing his good fortune, he'd prevent his fellow tribesmen from becoming envious. Some say passing these phallic symbols around is the father's way of reminding everyone that he had a significant part in this event, too—it's his way of pointing out to his men friends that he's strong and virile. Whatever the meaning, it's a fun way for dad to spread the good news. He doesn't have to smoke them; passing them out is what matters.

Consider participating in a baby blessing and include your other children if you have them. Many religious traditions wash the baby or sprinkle water on his head as a symbol of purity to honor the beginning of spiritual life. Christening is a welcoming of the baby into God's community. Frequently the baby is dressed for this in a white gown. A congregation I know of in Seattle fills a book with prayers and greetings signed from church members and presents it to the parents at the baby's spiritual dedication. Since sugar equals sweetness and goodness, some traditions put a dab of honey or sugar on an infant's tongue to ensure a sweet-tempered child.

If you are not members of an established religion, consider a ritual at home. Set out a few special items that have significance to your family. Perhaps a baby blanket or special outfit you'd like to bless. Light candles or paint stones with bright colors to represent each family member. Sprinkle heart-shaped confetti at your doorstep, make a paper chain, plant seeds or blow bubbles. Float flowers in a bowl. Say a blessing for your baby: "May this little one be blessed with love, health, and spirit. Include a blessing for yourselves: May we the parents be blessed with wisdom, strength, and generosity of soul. As we get to know each other and settle in, bless our family with gentle words and loving smiles." If you have other children, mention their names in the blessing and let them contribute.

Announce your baby in a quiet way or put a notice in the paper. Pass out cigars or lollipops, hang banners, call your friends or have your family wear pink or blue. Celebrating helps you absorb the magnitude and beauty of the event you've been waiting for.

Enjoy a Little Baby Talk

ave you ever noticed that when grownups converse with a baby, they talk in a soft, sweet, singsong voice? If the baby's crying, an adult will usually adopt a sympathetic tone to comfort and engage the baby. If the baby's laughing, the adult will immediately make happy, goo-goo sounds. This doesn't, of course, necessarily mean that the adult is behaving immaturely. They simply can't help it—it's like an automatic reflex and there's a sound reason for it.

Research shows that babies prefer soft voices and respond to the pitch of women's voices more readily than men's. From birth, a baby recognizes and is captivated by his mother's voice. By the age of three months, the baby can replicate a note his mother has sung to him. Moms express emotion through their voices and adapt the tone of their voice to respond to their baby's emotion. If the baby cries, the mom uses a different tone to comfort than she uses when the baby's laughing and wants to play. And by unconsciously changing her tone of voice, the mom gets better results—babies are soothed by soft sounds and excited by loud ones.

Talking to your baby before she is born is a good way to gain expertise in the art of baby talk, a form of playfulness. Playfulness brings thrills and happiness to parenting. Read poetry to your spouse and your baby. Laugh, giggle, be silly and spontaneous. Playfulness and laughter bring you closer to each other because you can't think when you're laughing, and that's such a relief after a hectic day.

Kenny puts his mouth close to his wife's belly and whispers, "Hi, little baby, this is Daddy." Annie was referring to her baby as "it" and told her mother-in-law, "I wish I could come up with a better way to refer to my baby." "Let's call your baby Rosebud," said the future grandmother, which was perfectly apropos, since Annie's maiden name is Rose. When Rick and Annie talked to their unborn baby they called her "Our

Rosebud." After their baby arrived, they named her Madeline, but Rick lovingly still calls her Rosebud.

Parents-to-be send lots of messages, "I love you." "We're so happy to be your parents." "We're going out for dinner now." "This is where your grandma lives." Candice said, "It seems like my baby pays attention when I sing—something in my body changes and my baby and I have a chat."

By talking to your unborn baby, you're letting her know she's already loved, which is an exquisite start. Chances are such a child will be optimistic and instinctively know that the world's a wonderful place.

> *When a woman participates with the process of childbirth, her whole existence vibrates with a new life; a new being is born. She becomes a vehicle of the divine. She becomes creator. Every fiber of her being vibrates with a new tune; a new song is heard in the deepest depth of her being. She will be ecstatic.*
>
> —Osho

PAMPER YOUR BODY

our body is a temple, the divine vehicle through which this new life will arrive, so you need to take good care of it. When you love your body, you listen to its demands, its hints, what it wants, and what it needs. And when your legs, feet, and toes scream for you to sit down, but you're already sitting down, it's time to treat yourself to a massage. In the final months of your pregnancy, it's probable that every cell and bone will be throbbing. That's because your body's been thrown off balance by your protruding abdomen, and your pelvic bones are shifting to prepare for delivery. Don't despair; massage can help, and there's a wide range of massage available, from Swedish, acupressure, and shiatsu (you don't even have to take your clothes off) to foot reflexology. There are even massage therapists who specialize in pregnancy.

A massage is therapeutic for both body and soul. As you're touched by a sensitive professional, your tense muscles relax, and corresponding emotions, which you may have been repressing, soften. In a safe environment, feelings and memories may surface, bringing a new awareness to your pregnancy. If you start to cry, please allow your tears. You don't need to explain. A lot is happening in your body right now.

Don't forget your feet! With so much emphasis on your midriff, it's easy to overlook your feet, but if your feet aren't feeling good, neither is any other part of your body. If eyes are the window to the soul, then feet must be the doorway to the body, because when a trained person touches your feet, your whole body sighs in satisfaction. If you haven't been taking care of your feet, at least in your ninth month indulge yourself. Sit with your feet up and soak them in a combination of warm water and lavender or orange blossom oil, then afterward try a gentle foot exercise by wiggling and stretching your toes. Personally I think a pedicure and manicure are necessities for all expectant mothers—the service ought to be available right outside the doctor's office as part of the visit. And please don't wait to wear reasonable shoes. As one mom four days past her due date told me, "In the end my feet are so swollen I gladly wear comfy earth shoes."

There are other things you can do to make your body feel better. Swinging in a hammock (although you might not be able to get off it without help) has restorative powers. One mom told me that a hammock was the best purchase she had ever made, since lying in it was the only way she could sleep on her tummy, and, after the baby was born, it saved many restless nights. When the baby wanted to be near or needed to be fed, they'd curl up together in the hammock and both be gently rocked. In order to get a good night's sleep, you might try what Ellen did. "I bought two full-length body pillows so I could prop up all my body parts that were dragging."

Wear clothes and lingerie that feel good. Nothing spoils a good day quicker than a bra that pokes or panties that cut off circulation, so, from the beginning, get undies that fit. Buy color-coordinated pairs if you can, because although it hasn't been scientifically tested, women in the know have insisted that wearing matched sets will have a positive effect on your psyche.

> *My daughter's birth was the incomparable gift of seeing the world at quite a different angle than before.*
>
> —Alice Walker

PREPARE FOR THE NESTING URGE

Sometime around your eighth month, you'll enter the "clean, rearrange, and decorate" stage—also known as the nesting urge. You'll know you've hit it when you find yourself staying up past midnight to throw away things you've been saving for years, when mundane tasks become thrilling and you feel like a creative genius as you dust the baseboards, scrub the top of the refrigerator, and vacuum all your lamp shades. It's when, out of the blue, you reorganize closets, iron clothes, or wash windows and hum "Whistle While You Work."

The nesting urge is strongest for first-time mothers, although experienced mothers have told me funny stories of their urge. Since they knew it was coming, they prepared by buying cleaning aids in advance. For when the nesting urge strikes—it's been known to hit before dawn—nothing is worse than wanting to rearrange your cupboards and discovering you have no shelf paper. With a little bit of preplanning, you can avoid a false start and be ready when the colossal cleaning bug strikes. Make a list of all the things you want to get done and match up the corresponding cleaning aids you'll need. Sounds obsessive, I know, but Karen the mother of three—with another one on the way—says, "That way you'll be less frustrated and complete projects that won't bother you until you're pregnant again." Clara was ordered off her feet for complete bed rest during her seventh month. So her friends organized a cleaning party along with a baby shower, and put the nursery together while Clara directed from her bed and folded diapers.

It seems that some husbands get the nesting urge, too. John remodeled a bathroom, Mike built shelves in the closets, and Mark refinished a rocking chair. Shelby thought the urge had passed her by, because she was overdue and hadn't cleaned a thing, then one afternoon she started cleaning the den and didn't stop until she'd reorganized the basement junk room. When she demanded that her husband clean the garage and make a trip to the dump, and he said he would, "After I wash and vacuum both cars," she knew they were about to deliver.

The nesting urge has a significance other than preparing a clean house for your baby. For your husband perhaps it's a way to be involved other than just standing by. For you, as labor approaches, bringing on a subtle restlessness, and your energy starts to peak, being active is a way of letting off steam that keeps you from feeling anxious.

I also think the nesting urge has a spiritual dimension to it. While some folks insist that there's nothing redeeming about washing dishes or scrubbing the bathtub, I don't agree. We've all heard spiritual teachers tell us of the joy and meaning in doing simple, everyday tasks—tasks that keep your family going. The Buddhists talk about the satisfaction of chopping wood and carrying water. What better way to express your gratefulness for your family than keeping one's home in order. Take a moment as you dust the furniture to acknowledge how blessed you are to have a piece of furniture to dust. As you put a load of laundry in the dryer, imagine your loved one's face and, as you prepare the evening meal, pour your love into it. Do your chores with a grateful heart. When no one seems to notice how much effort you are extending, remember that when your children are grown and have a home of their own, they'll look back with fondness at the loving energy you gave to transform their house into a home.

The nesting urge has a purpose to it, and when it hits you can't sit still. There's excitement in the air as if something special is about to happen—and it is.

Pregnancy is getting company inside one's skin.

—Maggie Scarf

ℒet Him Take Care of You

any a woman assumes that if her husband loved her, he would know exactly what she needed and wanted without having to be told. Perhaps you think this way, too, and, when your husband doesn't give you what you think he ought to, you feel hurt. When he sees that you are hurt, he doesn't have a clue as to what went wrong. It's a losing cycle that you can avoid when you learn to identify what brings you comfort and ask specifically for what you need. You spend a great deal of time caring for others, so, when it comes to asking for what you need, you may not know where to begin. In fact, sometimes when your husband asks, "Is there anything I can do for you?" you can't think of what you'd like.

You probably like to be pampered once in a while, but in the past have considered being taken care of a luxury, not part of your routine. Now, however, you find that you are feeling vulnerable. Your emotions and identity are in a state of flux. When that happens, pampering from your husband lets you rest and feel safe. You need to be treated with kindness and be catered to. Not because you can't do it for yourself, but because you need time to rest and find a stable footing.

Just as your baby asks for your attention by crying, you must ask your husband for what you need. But you don't have to wait until you're so overwrought that you must cry to let him know you need help. Communicate with your husband about your feelings of needing to be cared for more often. And let him know how he could pamper you in a way that is meaningful. Ellen loved the townhouse clean and neat, but her husband didn't like doing it. They talked it over and he volunteered to pay for a housecleaning service once a week. This took a lot of pressure off of both of them. Now instead of fretting and tidying up the messes, she has more free time to rest.

Ask yourself what household tasks you want to share so that you don't get bogged down with it all. Make a list of what needs to be done daily and weekly so that you and your husband can go over the list and divide the chores. What else do you need in order to feel cared for? Make a list in your journal. Does breakfast in bed appeal to you? Time alone? Perhaps a date once a week with your husband? Do you like him to cook dinner and do the dishes? Would you feel cared for if he waited on you while you read the paper? Is there anything else you need? Perhaps you'd like to have your husband's undivided attention for an hour each evening. Whatever you prefer, be sure to let him know.

Letting your husband care for you in these ways can be frightening. It's scary for many women to let themselves be so vulnerable. However, when you allow your husband to meet your needs, the trust between you grows.

> *It is common for expectant mothers to believe that having complex and conflicting feelings about their pregnancies makes them somehow "bad." But it does not. It simply makes them human.*
>
> —Arlene Modica Matthews

Cut Down on Obligations

If you haven't figured it out by now, the realities of pregnancy and parenting are not like those dazzling pictures in magazines. You won't always be smiling, bouncing off to work in a designer maternity suit. You won't often be relaxing in a pink flowing gown, daydreaming of playing on the floor with your baby. (Actually some of your daydreams might be about the carefree days before you were pregnant.)

When the baby's finally here, he won't always look angelic, and your figure won't spring right back into shape, no matter how many sits ups you do. You'll barely have time for a shower, let alone time to put on makeup or iron a blouse. When you're pregnant you still have laundry to do, meals to cook, groceries to buy, a boss who makes demands, perhaps other children to care for. You scarcely have the energy to do it all now. Yet soon, on top of all of that, you'll be caring for a baby. No way around it— you've got your hands full for years to come.

If you're going to survive and be a pleasant human being, someone that your child, your husband, and you, yourself, can love, you'll have to cut out some things in your life. Before you throw up your hands and say there's nothing that I can eliminate, consider these questions: What household chores are you doing that aren't vital to your survival? What social obligations do you have that you don't enjoy? What commitments have you made that feel like burdens?

You might want to ask your husband if he would pitch in. Mike didn't realize that he wasn't doing his fair share until his wife got pregnant the second time and was ordered to bed rest. He had to do everything and was amazed at how much his wife did that he knew nothing about. He made a list of all the chores, and, when she was able they divided the chores, negotiating for the ones they wanted. They like the system and have kept it operating for several years now. Once you've made the list, go over it again and ask yourself: Can I cut this out of my routine for one week? If your answer is yes, highlight that item and put it on your "I'm not going to do" list. It's healthy to have at least a few items on your list—like "I don't do windows" or "I don't do potlucks." Follow your "I don't do" policy for a month and then redo your list. Once you get the knack of cutting down on obligations, you can always add to or subtract from your list to suit your fancy.

By eliminating unnecessary obligations, you give yourself a gift of taking life a little slower. When you simplify, you're able to enjoy your pregnancy more. Someday you'll look back and cherish the down time. If you practice this "I don't do" procedure while you're pregnant, you'll be ready when the baby's here. Then you'll be thankful you have the skill so that you can rock your baby instead of waxing the floor. Alice, the mother of twins, told me what she'd discovered when, out of necessity, she was forced to practice this skill: "My greatest stress comes from what I think I should be doing, not from what I'm actually doing."

When you've conquered the skill of "I don't do," you're ready to write a second list entitled "I do." Having developed the "I don't do" skill, you'll be able to make parenting number one on your "I do" list and mean it.

Childbirth is difficult, but holding the child makes the pain worthwhile.

—Marianne Williamson

Appreciate the Miracle

f you've ever decided to have a baby and got pregnant right away, if you've ever longed for a baby but couldn't get pregnant for months or years, if you ever wanted a baby but waited until the time was right, you know that having a child is more than biological.

Thousands of babies are born every hour, yet having a baby is a miracle. It always has been and always will be. Pregnancy is not merely a medical condition. It's much more profound than all the laboratory tests, ultrasounds, fetal monitors, and hospital procedures. Pregnancy, labor, childbirth, and child raising, while definitely physical endeavors, are also mysteries. And although you wouldn't want to give up the safety net of modern medicine or technology, sometimes the wonder gets lost in the shuffle.

Expecting a baby opens your heart to joy. The unseen forces in the universe, things that you don't completely understand, are becoming evident. Life is sweeter. There's a twinkle in your husband's eye that wasn't there before; birds are singing; you're smiling more. When you're down in the dumps or have momentarily lost your spunk, you're not as discouraged; there's contentment in your soul. You can't explain it, but you sense it. A delicate shift is taking place—your heart is melting and you are becoming softer, gentler, more compassionate. Chloe described it best, "When I think of my children and grandchildren, a river of love flows through me."

You know you'll never be the same. You'll go to crazy lengths for the sake of your baby—she's your top concern. You'll forgo wine with dinner; if the doctor orders it, you'll give up chocolate and stay in bed for weeks; you'll lose sleep to rock him when he cries; and someday you'll stay up through the night to put his first train together.

When you carry your baby for nine months and are present as she or he comes into the world, you know you've been touched by a miracle. But it doesn't stop there. The miracle continues throughout your life. You've been given a glimpse of eternal goodness, and, to be worthy of the blessing, you must learn to love well. Through this helpless bundle, you will come to understand, in a way you never have before, that who you are, what you do, and what you say matters. If you're open to the sanctification that raising a child will bring, you'll be changed. Because you love a child, to the very best of your ability, the blessings keep on flowing. That's the gift. Appreciate it every day.

There are songs to be chanted, drums to be drummed upon, dances to
be performed, and tales to be heard. These thoroughly unscientific matters
of pregnancy give meaning and delight to what we are going through.
Pregnancy helps us come to our senses.

—Arlene Modica Matthews

Reflection

I remember having thoughts such as, Well, I'm not going to do that . . . I'm going to do this . . . I'll do such and such. As if they were incantations that could prevent me from doing the dreaded unknown that would change my sweet one to be into that awful little monster pulling cereal off the shelf in aisle three.

—Jean Gabrielle Theisen

Without a mother none of us would be here and without the feminine qualities of intuition, receptivity, patience, creativity, and generosity of soul, the world spins out of balance. Having a baby and nurturing a child is the manifestation of being a woman; keeping your feminine self strongly alive is the perfect gift.

Shape Your Parenting Philosophy

 teach many parenting classes each year, and I am struck by the large number of parents who have never thought about their personal parenting philosophy. Most never discuss, even with their spouse, their views on parenting. Instead, they naively assume that the two of them will magically adopt a unified approach. Frequently, when a joint decision is needed, they discover that they have conflicting outlooks.

When I ask parents on what basis they make decisions, they give me a wide variety of explanations from: "I had no choice," "It worked for my parents," to "It seemed like a good idea at the time," or "I let her decide." They come to conclusions in vague ways—"Because the neighbors do it this way," "My parents did it this way," or "I didn't want to do it the way my parents did." Without a conscious framework from which to begin, they have no parenting goals; they stumble and hope it all works out.

Before your newborn comes home, you will be making all kinds of determinations about his or her care—everything from whether or not to breast-feed, what kind of day care, finances, working schedules and so on. Forming a parenting philosophy will guide you as you consider each individual action you take; it points you in the direction you want to go; it helps you keep on track.

Before my daughter was born, I knew that I would be making thousands of decisions on her behalf, which felt overwhelming, since I'd never been a mother. I had my own parents as an example, but I knew I wanted to do some things differently and wasn't sure how to go about it. I asked myself what I wanted to accomplish as her parent.

The parenting philosophy I devised and still use today is: I will strive to raise a child who knows herself and feels good about who she is, so she can soar as an individual, enjoy her life, and make a contribution. I also wanted her as an adult to *want* to come to visit me. In order to do this, I placed my emphasis on building a loving relationship between us. By forming my philosophy, I had a framework from which to bounce all my decisions—easy and difficult. Even now, when I'm faced with a parenting dilemma, first I ask myself how what I'm trying to accomplish fits with my philosophy. Is what I'm about to do congruent? Will it help me reach my goal?

You can start forming your philosophy by considering these questions and talking them over with your spouse: What kind of parenting did you have? Did it feel good to be a member of your family? Did you feel as though you were living with people you could trust? Could you share your thoughts and feelings? What do you want to keep from your parents' child-rearing practices? What do you want to change? How will you make those changes? When you arrive at your philosophy by carefully considering these questions, you have created your most useful parenting tool.

Each time you're at a crossroads, check out how your decision fits with your parenting goals. You want your choices to be compatible with your philosophy. You can modify your philosophy as your family grows and changes, of course. The important thing is to start discussing with your spouse how you want to parent. The more you are able to do this, the more harmonious, joyful, and rewarding your life as a parent becomes.

A baby is Mom and Pop art.

—Patricia Warner

$\mathcal{S}$EEK REASSURANCE FOR YOUR FEARS

You're so glad to be expecting and don't want anything to go wrong, but you worry that something might. The unspeakable question runs through your mind, "What if something is wrong with the baby?" The fear haunts you now and then, and you try to shake it by reminding yourself that you and your husband come from healthy stock. You're cautious, careful not to do anything to harm your unborn baby. You know that the vast majority of women have uncomplicated pregnancies and healthy babies, and yet you worry: Will my baby be okay if I play tennis? Did that glass of wine I drank before I knew I was pregnant harm my child?

Every mother has fears. Worries are common, but don't torture yourself by fretting in secret. If you let someone in on what you're struggling with, you'll probably get good pointers and encouragement. You don't have to bear all these burdens by yourself. When Michele fell down the stairs, she was worried that the fall might have hurt the baby. Yet she was also embarrassed that she was overreacting; after all it was only three stairs. But since the baby's welfare was more important than her pride, she called her doctor, who reassured her that pregnant women fall all the time. "Your center of gravity has shifted, and, until you adjust, you're apt to be a little clumsy. Falls seldom hurt the baby," he assured her, "but take it easy for a few days."

Ann had an ongoing fear that her child would be born with a defect. When she mentioned this, friends and relatives would caution, "You shouldn't think such thoughts." She fretted alone for seven months. "I wanted to talk it over, but friends got upset when I did. Fortunately, the baby was perfect, but my pregnancy would have been more enjoyable if I could have talked about my fears."

Family and friends might be too close to hear your darkest fears. If that's the case, a counselor, nurse, or experienced mother might be just the person to listen. When you acknowledge your fears and talk things over with someone who has faced the same dilemmas, your fears will fade more quickly. Meg was forty-two when she became pregnant. The first thing she did was arrange through her doctor to speak with a genetic counselor about her concerns. Rather than denying her fear and letting her anxiety destroy her happiness, she became proactive in finding the answers to her questions. Throughout her pregnancy she had occasional spotting. The doctor reassured her nothing was wrong, but each time she insisted on making an appointment to be checked in person. She didn't want to waste time and energy worrying, so she was assertive about facing her fears and finding solutions if needed. If you are worried about the health of your baby, you can be assertive with your health care providers. Isn't that what they've been put here for? Ask them directly, "What are the chances that my baby will have something wrong?" Ask your doctor about an amnio and an ultrasound. Educate yourself as to what is going on inside your body. Visualize a healthy baby growing inside.

If you've spoken with your doctor, confided in a trusted friend, and still you're caught in an endless cycle of fret and uneasiness, you could be stuck in an incessant circle of apprehension, imaging scenarios of disaster. Mind dramas are a habit that you can overcome by setting aside twenty minutes each day to do a simple worry-reduction exercise. Cut twenty-five small strips of paper. On each strip write one worry. Then, one by one, read over each strip and ask yourself: Can I can do something about this today? If the answer is no, put it in the no pile. If the answer is yes, put it in the yes pile. When you have gone through all the strips, throw away the no pile. In the remaining pile you have strips of paper with worries that you can do something about today. Put them in order of which worry you will act on first, second, and so on. Then take the necessary action. Repeat this exercise daily. You will become very good at sorting out which worries require action and which worries need to be thrown away. Eventually you won't need the strips. The skill will be automatic.

TUNE INTO YOUR INTUITION

Your mothering nature begins to emerge when you're pregnant and your intuition begins to bloom almost as quickly as your belly. Indeed, many women say, "I knew the exact moment I got pregnant—I just had a feeling."

Mothers' intuition is a hunch, a premonition, a funny little gut feeling, a clue that "comes out of nowhere." Intuition is your special way of knowing whether you need to take action or whether it's wiser to wait for the answers to unfold. With your intuition working, you'll be able to relax, knowing that you can rely on yourself to point the way. As my friend Katy said, "I didn't tell anyone, but I had a feeling I was having a girl, and I did." Although you might not be as certain as Katy was, your intuition can point you in directions worth exploring. On the surface, the path may not always be clear, but if you tune in to your intuition you'll have a sense of what's best for you and your baby.

Intuition is good for deciding many things, from finding the right doctor and choosing a birthing method to knowing what to eat for lunch. It's very easy to tap into your intuition by paying close attention to your body signals—a sinking in your chest, a pit in your stomach. When you get that inner feeling signaling "this doesn't feel good," consider following your own feelings. Your friends may encourage you to use their doctor, but you have a feeling he is not right for you. You can't explain, you just feel it. Follow that feeling and chances are you will make the better choice for yourself. Laverne did just that, and not only found a doctor she liked, but met a nurse in the office who gave her a lead for a part-time job demonstrating educational toys. Your intuition is your personal advisor and guide.

You can learn a lot about mothering by watching other mothers and grandmothers. Some women have taken care of small children, while others have never held or rocked a baby, yet even first-time mothers learn quickly what they need to do. When the diaper needs changing, a mother does it even without having any practice, and, when it's time for the baby's first bath, she goes bravely forward, figuring it out step by step. That's intuition.

Your mothers' intuition puts you in touch with your baby and tells you what's needed. And even though you may not know exactly what to do for a colicky baby or a baby with a fever, your intuition will guide you to get advice from your doctor or your mother. Use your intuition in conjunction with old-fashioned advice and parenting classes, and you'll be able to sort through all the information and decide what's best. Then you'll have the sensitivity toward your baby that only a mother has.

Observing the world through your intuition becomes easy with just a little practice. For one minute each hour, be quiet and check in with your body for intuition clues and listen to your hunches. Then follow the messages. Chances are they will lead to something good.

> *I imagine the moment of quickening as a sudden awakening of my own being, which never before had life.*
>
> —Evelyn Scott

$\mathscr{S}$TEADY YOURSELF FOR TESTS

rom your first at-home urine test to the blood test in the doctor's office, you're going have a lot of tests and examinations. Some women get used to them, and others never do. There are so many tests that you'll need to talk with someone you trust to decide which ones are right for you.

It's routine to be examined by your obstetrician or midwife monthly until thirty-two weeks, then every two to three weeks until the ninth month when your visits are weekly. You'll be weighed, asked to pee in a small cup, and have your blood pressure taken at every single visit. You'll have so many vaginal exams (not every time) that you'll begin to bear them with equanimity. Nancy hated weighing in, because even when the nurse didn't give her a lecture, she gave a disapproving eyebrow raise. To avoid the unpleasant scene, Nancy scheduled her appointments to take place before she ate. Then afterward she headed for the donut shop and devoured a half-dozen minia-ture blueberry donuts. She tried them after the baby, but they never were the same. Maybe the nurse's censure made the donuts taste better.

Most women have an ultrasound at around sixteen weeks. It's fun because it gives you the quickest results. It pins down your due date, tells if you're having twins, can spot a penis (if you don't want to know the sex, tell them to keep it to themselves), and picks up any complications. Victoria didn't want to know her baby's sex, because knowing would spoil the surprise. Her friend, the mother of two, joked, "Are you kid-ding? With kids the surprises are just beginning."

Seeing proof of your baby is a peak pregnancy experience. Bring your husband and Kleenex with you—if he doesn't gets tears in his eyes, you can be fairly sure he'll at least have a lump in his throat. Schedule it early so the two of you can go to lunch afterward. You might not let yourself be excited until you've had the ultrasound, because you fear that something might be wrong, although the chances of that are slight. When you get the results, you can spend the next six months without worry.

Women over thirty-five also usually have an amniocentesis at sixteen weeks to diagnosis Down's syndrome or other genetic disorders. This test is a big deal emotionally. You'll be scared because you've heard that the needle itself can cause miscarriages (although the chances of this happening are very low), and, even though the odds are in your favor, you'll probably worry that something might be wrong. And then there is the waiting for the test results, which takes a week to ten days. Tests are given in a sterile environment and often by a technician you never met. For them it's routine, but for you it's far from routine. There are lots of other tests you could have—a glucose screen to assess risk for diabetes, a non-stress test, or a chorionic villi sampling. Whatever they are, chances are you're going to feel apprehensive in advance; drained and emotionally wrung out when they're over. Usually there is only slight physical discomfort, but the emotional upheaval can be hard. You might experience a general sense of sadness or unease—a soul malaise. You're reminded of the fragility of life.

Tests are for your body, but while you're going through them, you need to care for your soul. This can be very simple—a recognition of the importance of these tests for you and a silent prayer that everything will be okay: I've decided to have this test, but I'm scared and I want everything to be okay. Hold my hand, cradle my heart, be with me.

Take a support person with you. If your husband can't come, choose someone who understands the emotional wear and tear of such a day and whom you don't have to entertain. Wear something comfortable. Don't pack your day with errands. It's a strain for your heart and soul, and, even though the results are in your favor, it's not uncommon to feel weary when they're over. After you're done, if you want to spend the rest of the afternoon staring into space, lounging on the couch, or vegging out in front of the television, that's exactly what you need.

REFLECT ON MOTHERHOOD

nce your baby is here, you'll be so busy being a mother that you won't have a moment to ponder the big questions about what it means. Your every waking thought will focus on your baby, and your life will be a continuous cycle of diapering, feeding, burping, bathing, and napping. If this is your first child, it's hard for you to grasp how much your life will change and how much energy you'll soon be giving. If you already have a child, you know how all-consuming mothering is—a twenty-four-hour-a-day investment. To give you an idea of just how consuming it is, I read a study that found that the brain waves of a mother and her nursing infant are as close as those of identical twins. You've got baby on your mind.

But becoming a mother is not just about the baby, it's also about you—and now is the time to think about your role. You already are different. There's a shift taking place not only in your body, but in your psyche as well. Now you're responsible for another soul.

Motherhood is more than a role, more than feeding, clothing, and sheltering your child. It's protective animal instinct. It's unselfish giving. It's also about discovering a new dimension to your love. Mothering is about love, to a depth and magnitude that eternally wraps you with sweet concern for another. A mother never gives up, she's always available, and, as your baby grows, you'll discover a strength and compassion within you that you've never felt before.

What kind of mother do you want to be? Think about your own mother and about your relationship with her. Remember as far back as you can. Gaining insight into your mother's experience of mothering gives you understanding of your expectations and style. This is a good time to look over all the baby pictures—hers and yours—and reminisce. Perhaps you've heard stories about what life was like for her when she was expecting you. Imagine how she felt when you were born. How did she greet you? How did her life change after she had you?

Our vision of mothering is shaped by our own experience of being mothered. By the time you reach adulthood, you realize that your mother—although she did the very best she knew how to do—was not perfect. She probably took the best of what her mother gave her, improved on it, and gave it to you. Now you will take the best of her and give it to your child. What did your mother do that you would like to incorporate into your mothering? What qualities do you want to pass on to your child? What are the pitfalls you'd like to avoid?

Perhaps your relationship with your mother was abusive or extremely painful. If that is the case, you might find it difficult to consider these questions. But if you proceed slowly, you'll discover what changes in your mothering you'd like make. Then you can begin to heal from your childhood wounds and stop the chain of hurt and fear from continuing.

Perhaps your mother has died, and you're saddened that she's not here to share in the joy of her grandchild. It's okay to cry as she comes to mind. Remember that she has a permanent place in your heart, and you can connect with her loving spirit at any time. If you haven't already, consider gathering pictures of her and writing a story about her in your baby's baby book.

As you reflect on these things, remember that motherhood is also about happiness and optimism. A cheerful mother is a blessing to a child; her presence offers joy and hope. Take every opportunity to enjoy your life, find the silver lining, and spread your love around. A lighthearted mother gives her baby a reassuring view of life and an abiding well-being. A baby blessed with such a mother is surrounded with grace.

Meditate on the Path You've Chosen

otherhood is really the oldest profession and the highest calling anyone can aspire to. It requires the organizational skills and leadership that well-paid CEOs respect. As you nurture your newborn, there are thousands of infinitesimal yet consequential decisions you'll be making: Should she sleep in our bed? Should I pick him up when he cries? Later, as you guide your child on the road to independence, you'll have many questions to consider: Shall I work full-time? Who will care for my child? As a mother, you'll be making decisions hourly that affect the growth and development of a human being; you're responsible in countless ways for the life of your child and for the welfare of your family. It's a substantial position with lasting consequences.

Mothering never stops. You can't do it a mere eight hours a day, then go home for the evening. You can't squish it in between your career and your favorite pastime. You can't leave it behind for a moment. You don't get mothering breaks for lunch, to take a shower, or to read a book. The well-being of your baby is always foremost in your mind. Your child has a permanent place in your heart. From now on, at the core of who you are, you're someone's mother.

Morning is a good time to meditate on what this all means to you. Morning is a time of awakening when you can watch and witness the thoughts pass through your mind without making judgment. For five to ten minutes each morning for the next few weeks, quietly center yourself and become attuned to your mothering nature. In these moments do nothing, just let yourself relax into your being. As you empty your mind of distractions and allow what's in your heart to arise, you'll find who you are as a mother. You can ask yourself a specific question and let the answer come to you: What does it mean to me to be a mother? What is my vision for our family? What qualities do I admire in a mother? Meditate on one question at a time and you'll find that not only are you more relaxed, you're better prepared to face your day.

During your morning meditation, you reconnect with your feminine nature, which needs nourishment, yet so frequently gets neglected in the rush of daily routine. When you're pregnant and after your baby is here, it's so easy to fill your life with activities, responsibilities, and doing that the essence of who you are gets pushed aside and lost in the shuffle. When that happens, a melancholy, an uneasiness, and a longing settle in your soul. Partaking in a morning meditation can prevent that melancholy from expanding and sapping your energy.

Meditation is a mirror that reflects your original feminine being. When you catch a glimpse of the deeper nature of mothering, then mundane tasks of child care have new meaning and significance. As you come to appreciate the feminine qualities of warmth, serenity, contentment, kindness, compassion, and receptivity, you understand that your feminine qualities are what will make you a wonderful mother. Deep within your soul you know that you will put the needs of your child above your own, and, even though popular culture insists that this is not necessary or even valued, as you meditate on the path you've chosen, you find that your deepest longing is to care for and nurture your child.

With this clarity of vision, you have tapped into the source of abundant strength and healing. Whenever you are out of balance, melancholy, or troubled, you can call upon your feminine spirit to restore your soul. Creating the connection between your feminine self and your ability to mother will give you a reverence for yourself as a woman and as a mother.

ℛEKINDLE SEXUAL PASSION

f all the topics you might want to talk over with your husband, pregnant sex is probably the most awkward. But since pregnancy adds a new twist to your relationship, it's worth your consideration. If you and your partner are on the same sexual frequency, you're fortunate, because many of the couples I spoke with told me that the biggest difficulty when it came to sex was that one wanted more and the other wanted less. Pregnancy can turn your libido upside down. Some fathers are more turned on and others are repulsed; most couples are somewhere in between. For Glenn and Melissa, things went well most of the time, except when Glenn wanted sex and Melissa wanted sleep. That was in the first trimester. By the second trimester, she had so much sexual energy, he thought he'd died and gone to heaven! It was the opposite for Elaine and John. "I couldn't imagine having sex with my baby in there," said John.

It might be comforting for you to know that according to experts, pregnant wives underestimate how sexually attractive their husbands still find them. Perhaps it's because a curvy full body is erotic, perhaps it's because he feels powerful knowing he's created life. Even so, it's likely that you and your partner will be out of sync sometime during the nine months of expecting, as well as after the baby comes home.

You might be picking up that your husband, who once treated you as the sexiest woman in town, is no longer aroused by you. He isn't likely to admit to this, however, because he knows it would hurt you. It takes some men a period of adjustment to get used to thinking of their wives as both mother and lover. If you suspect this is the case, you might open the topic by saying as Rebecca wisely did, "Honey, if you aren't turned on to me while I'm pregnant, it's okay. I know you love me, and I remember those wild nights when we were making babies."

Using a non-confrontational opening lets him know you'll try to stay calm when he's honest that he's not turned on by pregnant bodies. Some men just aren't, but as Clint and Rebecca found out, being able to share secret thoughts and feelings is a mighty aphrodisiac—besides there are many ways to be close and loving. No matter how much you love one another, you won't be on the same sexual wave length all the time. Fortunately there are some things you can do to rekindle sexual spontaneity.

Women get turned on with lots of sweet talk, and men get turned on by fewer words and more action. With this in mind, you might reach out to your husband with a quiet touch. Slip beside him on the couch, take his hand and slowly breathe, then without saying a word, wait to see what happens. He may be suspicious at first, but, if you're gentle, sweet, and patient, the juices will probably start following. Or introduce a dose of fun. Since pregnancy reminds some husbands that they have to buckle down and get to work to provide for their family, they become so intent on earning a good living that they forget about enjoying themselves. Margaret found that things really livened up when she whispered in her husband's ear, "I've never made love to a Daddy before." If you cultivate your sexual inclinations, who knows what can happen?

You can connect sexually in many ways—a massage with oil, candlelight, incense, or music might rekindle the passionate feelings from your courting days. Lying in bed in that wonderful spoon position—you on your side with your back to your husband snuggling next to you—is a sensuous arrangement. It gives your expanding body "belly room" while bringing your bodies close. Breathe in unison. Focus on his breathing, allowing your breathing to follow his rhythm (good practice for labor). Be attuned to each other's vital energy and pay attention to the points where your bodies touch. Feel his body next to yours—relax and melt together. No need to rush. Gentle waves of ecstasy will soon ripple through your bodies. In this transcended space, you've discovered again what it means to sleep together.

REACH OUT TO YOUR SWEETHEART

exuality is a substantial force in both your and your husband's lives. It's the biological drive that brought you together. It's the source of your creative energy, which gives you tremendous pleasure. Without it, you might find you've lost a certain spark, feel less alive and less attractive. So while it's important to consider his needs for sex and attention, it's just as important that you let him know about your desires for closeness, affection, and sex.

A new dimension of your relationship is unfolding now. It's bound to be perplexing and unfamiliar as you and your mate consider the intricate details. It's a complicated matter. Some women find it difficult to reconcile their sexual nature with becoming a mother. Deep within the unconscious is the belief that the wild, sexy woman and the nurturing mother cannot coexist. That unconscious belief impacts your behavior; as the two images clash, you may feel disconnected from your former self. Even the most free among us seldom think of our mothers as sexy ladies. You may wonder if it's possible to take good care of your baby and be in touch with the sexy lady.

In a society where thin women are looked on as the most sexually desirable, some women have a heightened feeling of shame and embarrassment as their breasts become larger and their hips broaden. How you feel about your pregnant body will affect him and what you think he thinks about your body will affect you. If that's not enough to throw you in a quandary, there's the puzzle of figuring out how your newly shaped body will fit with his. Add hormones to the mix and no wonder your sexuality is haywire.

Not since your teen years has your body been so alien. You can't recognize your own breasts (Zoe called them "the girls"), your waist is gone, and when you stand up straight you can't see over your belly to locate your feet. In some ways, it's a foreign body, and you might not feel sexy in it. If you're self-conscious about getting bigger, tell him so. Your partner is not on the same roller-coaster ride of emotions as you are, so he'll probably have a hard time keeping up with what you're going through. He may have understood you before you were pregnant without your saying a word, but now you'll need to talk things over more carefully.

Perhaps you want more cuddling and less sex. If that's the case, tell him so and why. It's a good idea to fill him in rather than withdrawing or pouting, hoping he'll take the hint. During these months of intensified feelings, the more you're able to talk to one another—without freaking out—the safer you'll feel to work things through. Talking about your sexual feelings (or lack thereof) and listening openly to what your partner wants to express will bring relief. As uncomfortable as talking about pregnant sex is, it's certainly better than pulling away and storing up walls of hurt.

To help you open the conversation, first you must do a half hour of homework. Draw a line down a piece of paper, making two columns. Label one column "sexy lady" and the other one "loving mother." In each column, list the characteristics that describe that aspect of yourself. When your husband comes home, show it to him and ask him to add to the list. Together write a description of yourself using qualities from both lists. Begin your description with, "I am_____." Ask your husband to read the description out loud. Then you'll both see that, fortunately, you don't have to give up the sexy lady to become a loving mother.

Great with child, and longing...for stewed prunes.

—William Shakespeare,
Measure for Measure

Cook Him Something Tasty

efore I tell you this true story, I would like to add a disclaimer. I don't advocate putting your own needs on the back burner all the time, and I know you need your husband to baby you once in a while too. Even so, it might be invaluable for you to consider the wisdom in this tasty tale.

Lydia, eight-and-a-half months pregnant, was having a week from hell. Everything that could go wrong was, she was tired but couldn't sleep, her skin was thin and stretched, and her ankles felt and looked fat. As pregnant women sometimes do, Lydia was taking it out on her husband. She's not sure how all the commotion started, but it probably had something to do with wallpapering the baby's room. Her body ached, and she could barely waddle, let alone find the energy to stay calm while hanging wallpaper with this man—the father of her baby—whom she suddenly found to be totally irritating. She knew she'd asked Neil twice to turn off the baseball game, but he swore he didn't hear. Reacting without thinking, she turned stony silent.

He could tell she was distraught and asked, "What's wrong?" She answered sobbing, "How could you not know?" She slammed the front door—on purpose—and headed next door with such determination that he knew he'd missed something.

While her neighbor, Cecilia, stood by and nodded, Lydia pointed to her belly, "Now I'm tied to him forever and he doesn't begin to understand me." Lydia's entire body shook as she moaned about the week's injustices, then she took a nap on the living room couch. When she woke up, Cecilia advised, "Honey, you'll feel better if you cook him something tasty." Now before you freak out and scream, "He should be cooking for her," consider Cecilia's added tip, "the kindness you show to him will circle back to you."

Lydia chose not to indulge in the "pitiful pregnant me syndrome" anymore that day.

She walked back home and helped Neil clean up the sponges, and sheepishly nodded yes when he asked, "Feeling better?" The next evening, she served their favorite comfort meal: meat loaf, corn on the cob, fresh lemonade, and strawberry shortcake. He did the dishes. Because she was able to reconnect with her fundamental loving nature, Lydia did feel better, and her week went smoother. The baby's room was done on time, the wallpaper looked great, and Nathan Isaac was a healthy eight pounds, eight ounces. Cecilia's the godmother. Oh, by the way, Lydia's glad Neil didn't turn off the baseball game that day. It was the biggest upset of the season, with the Mariners coming from behind by nine points in the fourth inning to win over the Angels by one.

> *There is a golden cord that ties a mother to her child. It is God's knowing that is placed within us. There is no one who knows as well as we do what our children want and need. We learn what they want, we learn what they need, by listening to them and watching them. They know and they will tell us.*
>
> —Marianne Williamson

TRY SOME BEAUTY TRICKS

ight now, each cell of your body is busy chugging away as a baby-making machine. Your body is housing a baby in a very tiny space, and, as magnificent as that is, it's also jarring as your body makes the accommodations. Unsightly blue lines just under the skin of your abdomen, spidery reddish lines on your thighs, and swollen varicose veins in your legs are just a few of the changes you'll notice. Your skin is stretched, your bones are supporting more weight, and your face might take on a brownish tint known as the pregnancy mask. Looking at your pregnant body and wondering if you'll ever return to normal is enough to rattle even the most sedate among us. With all that's going on, don't expect yourself to carry on as if it's no big deal. You deserve pampering.

Remember, most pregnancy changes fade and disappear after delivery; for now a simple beauty trick might lift your spirits. I asked a group of expectant mothers how they took take care of their pregnant bodies. This is their advice:

1. Sleep with lots of pillows. Invest in a long body pillow, and wash the cover in a gentle soap several times before you use it. That's because your skin might be hypersensitive to detergents.

2. Exercise. Since this is the exercise generation, you probably already know this, but it's worth repeating: If you want to feel less lumpy and dumpy, a gentle exercise program will get those mood-lifting endorphins flowing. Pregnancy is not an illness, so there's no excuse not to move. Check the local YWCA or hospital for pregnant exercise classes. Debbie, a maternity fitness instructor, says that "The purpose of exercise during pregnancy is to maintain your current fitness level. If you do, you will recover quicker from delivery and have the stamina during labor to go that extra mile if needed."

3. Stock the house with healthy munchies and try to eat a balanced diet. To ward off a late afternoon feeding frenzy and keep your sweet tooth in check, devise a satisfying substitute. Sally rolled small scoops of fat-free lemon sorbet in almonds and kept them in her freezer. Knowing she had a supply kept her from rushing to the store for packages of cookies. Janey drinks fresh squeezed carrot juice for energy, then, if she's still craving chocolate, she indulges. Amber advocates fruit smoothies. Claudia insists nothing is better than expensive chocolate: "If I'm going to eat chocolate, I go to a classy shop and get the exact two pieces I'm craving. Then I eat them alone, so I can pay attention." "Never gulp chocolate on the run," she adds.

4. Put your feet up every time you sit down to prevent them from swelling.

5. Take 20- to 30-minute catnaps. A longer nap will make you groggy. Try to take naps someplace other than your bedroom. If you can, take mininaps out of doors, under a tree. Fresh air clears your pores and renews your soul.

6. Twice each day, and especially after a bath or shower, rub lotion on your breasts, thighs, and abdomen. You may not prevent those pregnancy trademarks (stretch marks and skin tags), but you'll keep your skin baby-bottom soft.

7. Since your body temperature and metabolic rate rises, you'll probably feel warmer than usual; keep cool by sitting in a pool or tub of lukewarm water, or soak your feet and hands in cool water.

8. Have your hair washed and dried at a hair salon.

9. Buy a new pair of soft slippers or socks and wear them around the house for a foot rejuvenation.

10. Take a shower in the middle of the day.

BREATHE, BREATHE, BREATHE

ntil you enrolled in a childbirth preparedness class, you probably had no idea there were so many ways to move air in and out of your lungs—deeply, shallowly, panting, blowing, puffing, gasping. A Seattle group nicknamed their class the "Huffin and Puffin School." By the end of six weeks, they could all recite the do's and don'ts of breathing. In class the moms, dads, and coaches all practiced the most productive techniques so no one would hold their breath during a contraction. The inclination to hold your breath aggravates pain; regular breathing, like a soothing balm, gives you the will to go through the pain instead of struggling. And if Dad is holding his breath while watching over you, he gets tense and you absorb the vibrations.

Allison said, "Learning to breathe at class was great for my husband, because it gave him something to do, and it helped him to be able to help me." Patty agrees, "Breathing helped me keep from yelling at him." (You can use that skill for years to come.)

This brings up the subject of making noise during childbirth. I've read stories of Bush women on the Kalahari desert who go off by themselves to give birth and never make a sound. The smallest moan is a disgrace, a sign of weakness. Thank goodness the same is not true in our culture! Groans, moans, whimpers, guttural cries, or even a primal roar can bring a momentary respite. While some swear that ladylike breathing is the only way to go, others know the relief of deep moaning. When you get the urge to groan, sigh, or whimper, don't use up your energy trying to contain it, but remember, on the other hand, that yelling frantically will only deplete you.

Melanie learned self-hypnosis to distance herself from the discomfort of childbirth. Dana and Eric used acupressure techniques, and Jane developed her own special brand of relaxation. With her husband's hand on her forehead or the back of her neck, she felt watched over and protected. Melissa, on the other hand, warns, "In the throes of labor, you may not want your husband talking to you, let alone touching you, so caution him in advance not to take it personally if you snap when he comes near you." John, the father of triplets, says, "I was in awe of my wife, so when she got feisty I did whatever she wanted."

These nine months often seem like the longest wait in your life, and each contraction seems five minutes long, when in reality it lasts only a minute. Set a timer and see how long a minute is. By breathing and by focusing your attention, you can survive that can't you?

Relaxed and focused breathing is a healthy tranquilizer for all kinds of situations. When you're having blood drawn, close your eyes and pay attention to your breathing. Use conscious breathing to get through medical tests, while in the waiting room at the doctor's office or when standing in line to buy groceries. On days when you have too much to do, a moment of focused breathing helps you get centered and find some balance.

Remember, mothering is about loving your child enough to hang in there. Breathing helps you go the distance. Once you've been through pregnancy, labor, and delivery, you've shown you've got the stuff mothers are made of.

If pregnancy were a book, they would cut the last two chapters.

—Nora Ephron

Think Glorious Thoughts

here's more to preparing for a baby than stocking the nursery and checking nine months off the calendar. For a pregnancy experience that is full and satisfying, you must think great and glorious thoughts.

Thoughts are the architect of your world, and unborn babies absorb more than vitamins and minerals. Just as what you're eating affects your health, what you're thinking influences your feelings, which your baby absorbs like a sponge. It's just as easy to emphasize the positive and be happy as to think negatively and be burdened. Your thoughts can be nourishing or toxic, pull your spirits up or drag you down. Thinking this *is too hard* makes pregnancy a chore; thinking *I'm bringing in a child of God* accentuates the joy. The music you listen to, the movies you watch, the books you read, and the radio and television you tune in, can agitate you and make you nervous or refresh you and calm you down. So be watchful of what material, information, thoughts, and words you take in.

Take good care also to surround yourself with cheerful people. Joan's neighbor was known as Ms. Grumpy. She'd grumbled when she couldn't get pregnant, yet once she was pregnant complained that the holidays were ruined because she was due in December. She chose to breast-feed, yet ranted to everyone who'd listen how she was tied down. She harped and protested every step of the way.

You probably know a Mr. or Ms. Grumpy, who can't find anything pleasant to say and spreads grouchiness around. A little crankiness now and then is understandable, but you don't need a steady dose of negativism; you need inspiration. Make friends with smiling, laughing people, and you'll feel happy too.

Amy's convinced that whatever an unborn child is repeatedly exposed to will influence her personality and aptitudes. She introduced art to her unborn baby by strolling through galleries and museums. She reads stories about Monet and looks at pictures of his garden. Even though you're not quite sure you want to read scientific journals to ensure your child becomes a research scientist, it's worthwhile to consider what thoughts and influences you're letting encircle your life.

Fill your home with positive vibrations. Buy fresh flowers, fill a bowl with potpourri, put a rocking chair by a window. Do a daily attitude check and read words of inspiration, pray, and count your blessings. Give encouragement to your husband and your children. Spread happiness around and you'll feel positive. Being pregnant is a formidable undertaking, but, with a slight shift in your focus, you can laugh about the challenges.

Make a list of what you like to do for fun that takes only five minutes and then put five-minute fun breaks into each day. Ask your husband and your children what they like to do for fun that takes thirty minutes and add that to your weekly activities. These nine months are jam-packed with plenty of stuff that has to get done; everyone is better off when you balance it with big portions of fun.

Whenever a child is born . . . there the angels' chant anew the sweet tidings of glory and peace and goodwill.

—Hyman Enelow

$\mathcal{L}$ET YOUR PARTNER DO IT HIS WAY

f you have a tendency to always be in charge, you might want to think about letting go of this tendency, particularly during pregnancy. Learning to let your partner sometimes take over and do things his way will feel great as you wait for the baby to be born, and it will have lasting positive consequences as you parent together. He may not understand what you're going through, and you two won't always agree on how to raise the children, but including him in your pregnancy in a way that's meaningful to him will help you feel well cared for and will keep him actively parenting for years. The challenge for you is respecting his unique husbandly way of being involved.

You probably have an illusory ideal of the perfect father-to-be. You know, the model husband who eagerly goes to every prenatal visit, who thinks you're more beautiful with your pregnant waddle, who raptly watches the childbirth video you brought home, then wants to discuss it. Well, according to the fathers-to-be that I spoke with, that's not exactly how they'd choose to be included. While many husbands were excited about having children, the way babies get here made them queasy. Even though they might be sympathetic to nausea, mood swings, and sudden cravings, husbands just weren't very interested in bodily functions and fluids. Max was willing to drop everything and go the store for chocolate ice cream and peanuts, but hearing about stitches and episiotomies put him in a daze. Since men like to fix what's bothering you, it often throws them into a quandary when you're raving about stirrups, specula, and vaginal secretions, which they can do nothing about. Gary doesn't talk much or say what Courtney wants to hear, but he showed his involvement by baby-proofing the house, rubbing Courtney's feet whenever she asked, and serving her breakfast in bed.

There's a wide range of ways your husband can be involved, but, if you insist he do it your way or pout because he doesn't show as much enthusiasm about the childbirth classes as you, then he'll close down and move away.

When you ask your husband if he wants to attend a childbirth class so he can be your birth coach, and he nonchalantly shrugs with less enthusiasm than you expected, try not to be too disappointed. When you watch a childbirth video and you see that he doesn't seem as involved as the husbands on the tape, try not to compare, pester, or pout. He might be slightly squeamish and need time to adjust.

Your husband could get interested in an aspect of this event that you've never thought of. One dad, after seeing so many pregnant parents in his first childbirth class, was curious to find out how many babies would be born on the same day as his own. He calculated—based on the population at the time—that there are 7.5 babies born in the United States each minute or 10,800 each day. He set out to research what number would be given the same name, but the other dads convinced him that was going a bit too far.

If you want your partner to be a hands-on daddy, you need to practice by letting him show you how he wants to be included. Peter knew he'd blown something when Kathryn pulled away as he tried to snuggle closer. "Is anything wrong, honey?" Through sobs, she answered, "What do you mean you won't pay for your children's college education?" For a moment, he didn't have the faintest idea what she meant. Then he remembered the conversation with friends over dinner. "All I said was that I thought kids should have jobs and contribute."

As this example shows, just because he expresses a viewpoint different from yours doesn't mean he doesn't love you anymore. You'll have many hypothetical conversations, so don't freak out if you don't always see eye to eye. Sharing your different perspectives helps you find mutual solutions. From the pregnancy test through labor, your husband will worry, work, and wait alongside you—that's a comforting contribution. Let him show his connection in his own way.

CONSOLE YOURSELF WITH TEA

You know that you're loved, and you've probably gotten lots of attention. Still, there are those times when you feel crazy, forlorn, misunderstood, and downright lonely. Besides suffering from perpetual heartburn because the baby is sitting on your stomach, there are days when you feel abandoned and forsaken. When you suffer from the no-one-understands-what-I'm-going-through blues, you need natural remedies. Herb tea in a china cup with tiny sandwiches and a piece of chocolate on the side can soothe frazzled nerves more quickly than pep talks. If you've sworn off chocolate, strawberries and kiwi are a royal substitute.

There's a few remedies you should do without. Booze is definitely out. Don't use alcohol in any form to cope with pregnancy madness. Doctors disagree about exactly how much alcohol can harm the fetus, but all agree that it can cause serious birth defects. If you think you'll go crazy without a drink, definitely check it out with a medical professional. Smoking cigarettes or marijuana is also unhealthy. Non-prescribed medications may also be harmful. When in doubt, remember that whatever you put into your body, the fetus absorbs through the placenta. You certainly don't want a baby with a predisposition to using drugs, alcohol, or cigarettes.

While there have been no definitive studies linking caffeine and birth defects, caffeine is definitely not good for pregnancy nerves. It's a stimulant that increases the heart rate and blood pressure. Herbal tea, on the other hand, is an elixir extraordinaire. While coffee and caffeinated tea wind you up, herbal teas calm you. Since no two pregnancies and no two labors are alike, what works for your friends might not work for you. You'll need to experiment until you find the right tea therapy. Peppermint tea is good for morning sickness and nausea, and assists in digestion. Chamomile tea calms your nerves and aids in sleep. Leigh recommends iced lavender tea with lemon for headaches, and she eats unsalted almonds when she's shaky, cranky, or craving sweets. She carries almonds and a thermos of iced tea for afternoon breaks. Lots of water is good too. Leigh keeps a crystal goblet on her desk for water. She's heard that drinking raspberry tea daily one month before labor eases contractions. She drinks eucalyptus tea for colds and takes warm baths in rosemary tea to get rid of cellulite. She swears that beet juice cures hemorrhoids and prunes ease constipation.

I don't think you have to go that far, but if you live in a city with a hotel that serves afternoon tea, I strongly recommend treating yourself once during your pregnancy to high tea. Believe me, it will lift the cloud of gloom, and you'll feel like a princess for a week.

While high tea is a peak experience, there are other things besides food that are perfect for soothing your soul. Go to garage sales or browse through a garden shop. Almost any time of the year, you can start a window garden. In the fall, you can plant daffodil and tulip bulbs in a container at your front door. In the winter you can plant paper white and hyacinths in a bowl of pebbles. Digging in dirt and planting pansies, roses, or ornamental cabbage connects you to all living things and reminds you that the benevolent force that makes the grass grow, the flowers bloom, and the fruit ripen is within you, too.

A baby is God's opinion that the world should go on.

—Carl Sandburg

GIVE ATTENTION TO YOUR DREAMS

 veryone dreams, every night; even if they can't remember what they've dreamt. As we go through our days, deep feelings get triggered, and, when they're hard to verbalize, the unconscious mind mulls them over through symbols in dreams.

Dreams during pregnancy are often very powerful. So much is happening inside of you over which you have no control that no matter how happy and positive you are you're bound to be scared, too, if only because life will never be the same. This ambivalence often comes out in dreams. Mindy dreamed that she was lost in an unfamiliar city and couldn't find where she was supposed to be staying. She ran in circles around the same block with no one noticing. She woke up with her heart pounding, feeling shaky. She wrote her dream down and read it later. Thinking about it brought the realization that she was feeling helpless but believed she shouldn't tell anyone. Because of the dream, she decided to vocalize her feelings of being lost and unsure of who she'd be once she was a mother. As she talked about this with other new mothers and with her husband, she found her way of making peace with her new identity.

Dreams of having a deformed child are frightening, but not uncommon. Just because you dream that your baby will be impaired doesn't mean it will be so. Dreams of having a baby with something wrong means you're worried about that, not that something is wrong. Remember—you can't make it go wrong by dreaming it will. If you do have such dreams, go easy on yourself while you are awake. You are feeling the vulnerability of pregnancy and need not stuff those feelings down.

Jill dreamt that she had an exceptionally cute baby boy and then lost him at the grocery store. Instead of looking for him, she went home. In her dream she was not upset, but the fact that she remembered the dream so vividly disturbed her greatly. She was unable to shake it and felt so guilty that she talked about it with me in a counseling session. Jill's heart was set on having a girl, and although she tried prepare herself for the possibility of a boy, under the surface she was concerned that she wouldn't be able to love a boy. As she talked about her dream and her guilt about not wanting a boy, she came to accept that she could, in fact, mother a son.

Not all dreams have hidden messages; some are so straightforward they are obvious even as you're having them. Jodie dreamt she was having wild sex with her doctor—he just couldn't keep his hands off her—and she was enjoying it thoroughly. She woke up turned on. (Her sleeping husband got the benefit, even though she kept the dream to herself.)

One good way to chart your unconscious feelings about giving birth is to write your dreams down. As you look at them later, as Jill did, they can provide important clues as to where you are emotionally. To do this, keep a pen and tablet next to the bed, because if you don't record dreams immediately upon waking, chances are you'll forget them.

Some women get so good at taking charge of their dreams that they program them in advance or can change them in midstream. Regardless of how you cope with dreams, remember that erotic and nightmarish dreams as well as worried and ambivalent dreams are all normal. Talk about the ones that are upsetting, and, like Jodie, enjoy the others to the maximum.

> *I think of birth as the search for a larger apartment.*
>
> —Rita Mae Brown

$\mathscr{K}$EEP A POSSIBILITY JOURNAL

possibility journal is a storage place for thoughts, feelings, dreams, and longings. It is a place for wishes. It begins as a blank book with blank pages. As you write, draw, paste, and color, you turn a blank book into a possibility journal. And with that journal in hand, you can turn possibility into actuality. You can tell your story and fashion a vision. With a vision you have a road map and a direction for your life.

Pregnancy is about hope, hope for yourself and your child. Within every woman is a wellspring of vibrant energy that is stirred and unleashed when she is pregnant. By exploring your creative potential, you can unlock this power and find new determination. With determination, you can turn your hope into action. Let me show you how.

Women have children for many reasons, some of which aren't positive or noble. Some become pregnant by accident, others plan it because they're lonely, bored, or to fill a hole in their own hearts. Regardless of the reasons—noble or selfish—you got pregnant; you've been given an opportunity. Your possibility journal will be the guide to discover the opportunity, expand it, and grow as a consequence. You're having a baby for a reason. What is your purpose for bringing a baby to your family? Write your answer in your journal. Look deeply within and write as honestly as you can.

Every mother-to-be wants her child to take the best of her and become more. But not all of us accomplish this task. Some moms become jealous, fearful, or distracted; without a clear vision of themselves as mothers and women, they get off track. With a possibility journal, you can stay on course in your own life and guide your baby from birth to adulthood to become a beautiful, responsible, honest human being. I'm not talking about pushing. I'm talking about knowing yourself well enough that your child sees from your example that wishes do come true. He sees from your life what it means to accomplish something meaningful; by watching you she learns to live with joy and integrity. She will see your heart singing and is therefore free to sing her own songs.

What do you wish for yourself? Cut out five pictures from magazines that represent your deepest wishes. Paste them in your journal and write a sentence underneath. Now paste five pictures that represent what you wish for your baby. What kind of life do you want him to have? What do you want to teach her? What beauty do you want him to see? What actions are you willing to take?

Write down five qualities that you admire in yourself. If you have trouble, ask friends to help you, and write down what they say. Think about what you can do to enhance those qualities. Do you need to become a better person? In what way? Is there unfinished business from your past that needs cleaning up? With colored markers, decorate the pages any way you choose. Write a list of your favorite words, your favorite children's books, your favorite nursery rhymes, your favorite hiding spot. Write a poem for your baby and put the words in a vertical line. Or write a letter to your unborn child and tell her something silly, or write something from your heart.

Actions begin with hopes and wishes. Writing in a possibility journal turns hopes into vision, which, when ripened, evolves into action. That's your opportunity.

> *Don't forget that compared to a grownup person every baby is a genius.*
> *Think of the capacity to learn! The freshness, the temperament, the will*
> *of a baby a few months old!*
>
> —May Sarton

REMEMBER WHAT REALLY MATTERS

 hen you bring your baby home from the hospital, your house will spontaneously fill with so much energy that whenever your child is away your house will seem empty. And when you're away from home, you'll feel as if part of you is missing and you'll be anxious to get back. There's no doubt about it, as a parent, children matter most.

Taking care of a newborn is difficult. Almost every new parent has proclaimed, "No one told me it was this hard!" and "Nobody told me how rewarding it would be." Yes, it's difficult and complex, but you keep doing your best, because it's worth it. You may not earn a medal or a blue ribbon, but the recognition comes in a thousand and one ways. A pat on the chin, a smile, a giggle, a first word, a first step, a scribbled crayon picture hung on the refrigerator.

I once heard a story about Danny DeVito. Someone asked him how he got to be such a big movie star, because he certainly didn't have the looks for it. His response is worth considering. "My mother thought I was fantastic, the best kid around, she thought I was truly special, that I could do anything, and I believed her." Without your love, life for your child can easily be a struggle. With love almost anything is possible. The reward for a mother is in giving it and seeing it flourish.

Toni told me, "I feel completely different now that I'm a mother. Now what is most important to me is what kind of person I am. I used to be a material girl. Now all I think about is our baby. I want to be a better person so that I can be a perfect mother." We all know that as mothers we are not perfect, yet we long to be perfect. It's a natural instinct. The only way I know to achieve maternal perfection is by focusing on what really matters to you.

The most basic need of a baby is the security of loving arms and, a peaceful, safe home. A baby cannot grow into strong child without roots; with roots his arms can reach to the sky. You are now responsible for a baby. Responsibility really means your ability to respond not only to her physical needs, but her spiritual needs as well. On those days when the bathtub needs cleaning, there's not enough money in the bank, and you don't want to cook another dinner, it's hard to keep your spiritual perspective unless you have a simple reminder to get you back on course. Choose an item to help bring your awareness into focus. Perhaps a baby item such as booties, a package of seeds, or dried baby's breath flowers. Carry this small item with you and let it be a constant reminder of your highest purpose. Say a prayer daily, "Guide me, mother of the universe, to stay on course, to give my baby roots and wings." Whatever you do, do it joyfully and, cheerfully, pour your heart and soul into it, and you'll be a wonderful mother.

Lie in the sun with the child in your flesh shining like a jewel.... Let your life swell downward so you become like a vase, a vessel. Let the unknown child knock and knock against you and rise like a dolphin within.

—Meridel Le Sueur

$\mathcal{T}$AKE IN THE SPIRITUAL LESSONS

regnancy is an invitation to learn spiritual lessons that prepare you for the holy responsibilities of parenting. As you learn the lessons, you will find they contain a blessing that gives fulfillment to your pregnancy and subsequently to your life. While some lessons are obvious even to the uninitiated—going through the pain of labor to participate in the miracle of birth—others are more mysterious and require you to open your heart to find their meaning and purpose.

The first spiritual lesson of pregnancy is that you don't need to push the river. This is the lesson of allowing the life force to carry you—without your forcing and striving—to its natural completion. As a child, I spent many summer days with my friends floating on inner tubes down the Boise River. Our parents would drop us off up the river and we would float down to the park, where they would meet us. On hot days the river was full of rafts, tubes, and people of all ages. I noticed that people had different floating styles for getting down the river. Some folks jumped on their inner tubes, paddling and kicking as fast as they could. Others closed their eyes, lay back, and let the current carry them along. No matter what style they used, everyone arrived at the same spot. The only difference was some arrived sooner, others arrived a little later. But everyone got to where the river took them. This is true for your pregnancy too. You will get to where you're going.

When you find yourself driven internally to make your pregnancy something that it isn't, think of lying on an inner tube in the sun floating down the river. You will get to where you're going with or without a frantic effort. When you let the divine river of life carry you, you will enjoy the journey more. You can use this lesson throughout your pregnancy, during labor, and during your recovery from birth.

The second lesson is one of acceptance. You learn acceptance by saying: "Yes, yes, yes" with all your heart and soul to life's gifts as they are given. You may wish for a boy but have a girl. We've all heard stories of children who knew that their parents preferred a baby of a different sex. As the child grew, she felt inadequate because she was unable to fulfill her parents' desires. By the time your baby is born, you must let go of this idea for your baby's sake as well as your own.

Acceptance goes deeper than preference for a boy or a girl, and you know it. So we might as well talk about it openly. All parents pray for a healthy child, and for most parents this is what will be, but a small minority will have a child with a defect. It may be something as minor as a birthmark, or something more significant like a cleft palate. While this is devastating at first, parents faced with this situation find themselves blessed with abundant grace to see them through. If this should happen to you, know that you will be given ample emotional resources to tackle the problem.

All spiritual lessons call us to rise above our egos and our earthly desires. Perhaps the disappointments and heartaches are necessary for pruning our egos so that we can love without demands. We want our baby to be perfect, to be beautiful and brilliant, yet in the end, we find that we love our baby for the baby's sake, not for what she can do for us. Begin today by saying "Yes, yes, yes" with all your heart so that you, too, can receive the heavenly blessings delivered through the baby that you are given.

It seems to me that since I've had children, I've grown richer and deeper.
They may have slowed down my writing for a while, but, when I did write,
I had more of a self to speak from.

—Anne Tyler

WILLINGLY MAKE THE SACRIFICE

o be a parent is to let yourself in on a lot of sacrifice. Pregnancy in itself is the ultimate sacrifice as you offer your body, heart, and soul to your baby. However, pregnancy, labor, delivery, and parenting mean giving, giving, and more giving. It's giving when you don't feel like giving; it's loving when you don't feel like loving. To love your baby you must sacrifice your ego, your privacy, your free time, and your ideas of how you want things to be.

Sacrifice comes from the word sacred. When you give willingly and joyously, then what you are sacrificing becomes a sacred gift. When you bathe the baby, change the bedding, wipe a runny nose, or do your fifth load of laundry with a song in your heart, you are growing as a spiritual being. To do this is to enter into a state of gratitude, of thanksgiving for all the beauty and the grandeur in your everyday existence. When your baby moved inside your body, did you not feel the interrelationship between your souls, the sun, and the moon? Have you not felt life pouring from everywhere? When you give without joy, you are merely fulfilling your duty, but, when you give with a joyous heart, you are giving something sacred.

There will be times during your pregnancy and labor, even with loving people surrounding you, when you feel more alone than you've ever felt. Days of bones aching, hours of labor pains ripping through your skin, and nights of walking the floor with a crying baby when you're tired and weary yourself. You'll feel dried up and empty. This is the time when you develop spiritual courage, an inner journeying where only you can go. A journey so deep that you need guts and gumption to face the truth of your aloneness.

There is grief with pregnancy. It's the nature of things. Nothing is permanent. Life is dynamic; you know it when you're pregnant, for each day you're changing. But as you shed the old you, the new you emerges. Grieve quickly for what was and enjoy the newness and surprises of what is. Know that everything has a purpose. Pregnancy is full of countless contradictions. Pain and joy go hand in hand as the pain of labor is rewarded with the joy of birth.

It's a challenge to balance your needs with those of your family. Often you will put your wants and dreams on the back burner to care for your newborn. There are days when you barely speak to an adult and when you're too tired to even sleep. But please remember it's worth it, because you're only pregnant for nine months, your infant's only an infant for three months, and your baby's only a baby for a year.

The involvement between a mother and a child is based on this spiritual sacrifice. It's the deepest involvement you will have. You'll make many personal sacrifices for the sake of your child. When you're in the middle of labor you may wonder why you're doing this. But when they place your baby in your arms, you'll know that as much as you have given, you have received more.

There are one hundred and fifty-two distinctly different ways of holding a baby—and all are right.

—Heywood Broun

GROW WITH VIRTUES OF PREGNANCY

o be a mother means you are asking to be entrusted with the soul of an innocent child. It means that you are enthusiastic and ready to share all that you are and all that you have. It means that you will watch over the body, heart, and soul of your baby. Patience, compassion, truthfulness, generosity, steadfastness, gratitude, playfulness: These are the virtues of motherhood.

The true virtues have nothing to do with morality, but rather with wisdom. A mother is expected to be wiser than her child; she has to be. To be a wise mother you need the wisdom of knowing yourself well enough that you have room in your heart to love a baby who has colic, a dirty diaper, and projectile vomiting. It's being aware of yourself so that you are able to respond—to behave responsibly—rather than merely reacting out of an old pattern or fear.

To ready yourself, you must be willing and eager to cultivate the virtues of motherhood. To do so requires that you let go of self-centeredness and greed so you can fill your heart with gratitude and your mind with positive thoughts. You cannot fake these virtues or impose them on yourself. These virtues dwell within and arise from your spiritual core. To find them, you must be courageous and willing to do a spiritual practice (and to go easy on yourself when you fail—which you will).

Choose a meditation or a prayer that focuses on one of the virtues of motherhood. Begin with patience. Don't force yourself to be patient, but rather ask for patience to blossom within you. Patience means hope and trust without any hurry. When you want what you want right now, you are tangled in a knot of immaturity and you'll soon lose heart. You'll fly off the handle easily and lose your temper quickly. By allowing patience to blossom, you will respond with kindness and remain ever-trusting and full of hope. The paradox of patience is the less you force things, the more quickly they happen.

Next, consider the virtue of playfulness. Without playfulness, life is drudgery and work unbearable. But add playfulness to all you do, be it driving, weeding the yard, changing the beds, or parenting, and suddenly life is full of sparkle. You've opened the door of possibility, and your parenting is full of creativity. With a playful attitude, you bring out the best in your child.

For the next week, choose one virtue each day and let it be your meditation. Just thinking about the virtue—be it patience, playfulness, compassion, or gratitude—is enough to start it spreading. When you come to understand that your baby does not belong to you, even though she comes through you, that she has her own divine destiny, then you are a mother of wisdom. It's not your job to force, mold, or impose but rather to love as much as you can and become a beacon of positive virtues to emulate.

The tiny perfect fingernails and toenails astonished him the most. They were like small pink shells you scuffed up in the sands of tropical beaches, he whispered, counting them.

—Kathryn Hulme,
Annie's Captain

Surrender to the Process

regnancy is a process that invites you to surrender to the unseen force behind all life. When I think of pregnancy, I immediately think of gardening. I look at it this way: It is enough for each of us to plant a seed, provided that we care for it, but we cannot make it grow. We can't actually make a seed grow—a seed grows because of the combined force of our care and an unseen force in the universe that is the energy behind all life. That's the miracle of life. And the seed doesn't even have to struggle. We struggle much more than we need to. That is true regarding just about everything.

My grandmother was my gardening mentor. She said there was the joy of harvest, and that's a wonderful and exciting happening. But, she said, gardening also requires quiet diligence and respect for the whole process, and in a way that is just as satisfying. I was very young, and I loved it when my grandmother talked to me about all that. She had grown blind, but still she had one of the most beautiful gardens I ever saw. Being blind didn't stop her one bit. Yes, there can be many gardening disappointments and frustrations. Frost may come and wipe out the flowers, or rabbits may eat up your crop. That kind of thing is frustrating and hurts, but, if you're a real gardener, it won't stop you.

On your journey to becoming a mother, there can also be disappointments and setbacks. My friend Linda had two miscarriages before she carried her baby to term. After the second miscarriage, she was depressed and asked "Why me?" Many times she cried herself to sleep. She prayed for understanding, but she never understood. Then one fall day while walking in a garden with only a few summer blooms remaining, she stopped asking for answers and surrendered to her helplessness. "Life cannot be understood," she cried, "it can only be lived."

Mary wanted natural childbirth and had decided on a water birth. She made arrangements to have a birthing tub at the hospital—it took her months of preplanning. When she had an emergency cesarean, she was shaken, but since she didn't want her disappointment to interfere with her care of the baby, she talked it through with a close friend and her doctor. As she came to understand that the cesarean was performed to save the life of her baby, she was able to let go of her regret and not blame herself. We may think we know what is best, but often in pregnancy and childbirth we have to surrender to a higher wisdom—we can't run the show alone.

Surrender is the melting of your will, the letting go of how you think things should be in favor of stepping into the unknown and trusting the unseen life force that gives the tulips, daisies, roses, and daffodils their fragrance and color. When you surrender, you turn the outcome over to a higher force, having faith that the greatest good will occur. In that moment of surrender, your heart softens, your mind opens, and you are given the freedom to see clearly, without your own expectations clouding the view. It is in surrender where you meet your baby with unconditional love and fully embrace the spirit of the garden that is within you, your spouse, and your child.

> *In her own interest, every pregnant woman should make a habit of never entering a room without making a note of the quickest way of getting out of it and into either fresh air or a bathroom.*
>
> —Audrey Hull

$\mathcal{T}$REAT ALL YOUR CHILDREN LOVINGLY

he Gilberts wanted their new baby's arrival to be a family affair, but they knew five-year-old Sloane would need preparation to accept a little sister. They consulted books, talked to friends, and did everything the experts advised to help her feel included. They took her for a tour of the birthing center and peeked in the nursery. At the gift shop, they let her choose a rattle for the baby and pick out a baby doll for herself. They told Sloane stories about her baby days, looked at pictures, and reminisced. They said how pleased they were on the day she was born and said, "Mom and Dad are happy to have a new baby just like we're so happy to have you." They hoped for a smooth transition, but Sloane wasn't as sure. When she kissed her sister hello for the first time, she jumped down from the bed and told her grandma, "I don't want to be a big girl anymore."

Cathy made extra effort to included her seven-year-old stepson, "I want Parker to feel special as a big brother." Parker couldn't wait to be a brother. Cathy answered his question of "How does the baby get out?" with the response, "Through a tunnel." He patted her tummy and designated the bottom bunk for "my baby brother." He bragged to teachers and friends, "I'm going to see my brother born," which was news to Cathy and his father. But a week before the baby was due, Parker had a change of heart and confided in his dad, Joe, "I don't think I should be there when my baby's born." "Why not?" asked Joe. "Because babies are born naked, and if it's a girl I might see her virginia."

As these stories show, kids have a great deal of ambivalence about the new baby, so expect the unexpected and be patient. Your children are not so sure about sharing you. Do your best to answer their questions. Small children want simple, brief answers. Older children might feel embarrassed. Eleven-year-old Sydney screamed when she learned her parents were expecting, "How gross! Did you and Dad do it?" Speak to their feelings. They'll be worried that you'll love the baby best. Reassure them through your words and actions. Include them in the preparations—ask their opinions about names, the baby's room, clothes, and so on.

That's the easy part—now here's the bigger challenge. Although you're eager for them to get along, don't overdo it. Don't try to convince an older child to accept the baby. They'll do it at their own pace—it takes time. They probably won't like the baby immediately and will feel jealous. But don't let it get you down—it's a perfectly normal reaction. Never scold, criticize, or mock them for acting like a baby, sucking their thumb, or reverting to baby talk, Instead, hold them on your lap to rock and cuddle. Give lots of reassurance. Say, "I love you, oodles and oodles." Be lighthearted and respectful of their feelings, and the insecurity and rivalry will fade.

> *A new baby is like the beginning of all things—wonder, hope, a dream of possibilities. In a world that is cutting down its trees to build highways, losing its earth to concrete...babies are almost the only remaining link with nature, with the natural world of living things from which we spring.*

> —Eda J. LeShan

CONTEMPLATE YOUR PRIORITIES

id you ever in your wildest fantasies think that one day you'd be a budding expert on baby strollers and car seats? Once you debated the merits of social change; now you agonize over cloth or disposable. You fold and refold little shirts and sleepers daydreaming about a wiggly little body soon to be wearing them. Your favorite smell is baby powder. You weigh the merits of staying home to organize play groups and build sandboxes. You turn in your sports car for a van. Baby paraphernalia takes precedence over CDs and new dishes. You'd rather buy a wind-up swing and a high chair. The baby hasn't arrived, yet you're fascinated with building blocks and tricycles. You plan ahead and baby-proof the house with plugs in electrical outlets and a gate across the stairs.

Impending parenthood turns your priorities inside out and upside down, and it rearranges what you once thought was important. Once you thought in terms of a couple, but now that you're having a baby you start asking: What's best for our family? "My husband and I believed for years that we could have it all—career and family life," says Dorie. "Now with our second child on the way, neither of us wants to work the long hours our careers demand, so we're looking at our options."

We've all been indoctrinated with the notion that the modern woman is not happy unless she has it all—a loving husband, a successful career, happy children, and a cozy, well-run home. This image of what it takes to be a satisfied woman has become so pervasive that we accept the assumption that unless we have these four things simultaneously, something is amiss. We try to balance our family with work and squeeze in overtime while the kids are shuffled to the sitter. We stay up late to fold the laundry and read bedtime stories while falling asleep. We've become so adept at squeezing it all into our busy schedules that our perfect lives become blurred and we start to question our choices. We strive harder and harder to make things run smoothly, pushing ourselves to do it all and have it all, all at the same time. We think we should be able to do it all with ease; after all, we're women of the twenty-first century.

Women are indeed capable of most anything, but, before you push yourself to do it all, ask yourself if you really think it's wise to spread yourself so thin, to push yourself so hard. When your children are grown, how do you want them to remember their childhood? How do you want them to describe you? Ask yourself, "Do I want to rush right back to work? Do I want someone else to care for my baby?" Is it really possible to have it all, and, if you can, is it worth the pressure?

Many couples decide they have no options and believe it's hopeless to try a new way. They're locked into a lifestyle—trapped by limited thinking. Please don't let this happen to you. Deciding what's best for your family and how to achieve it is not always clear cut. You may want to stay home with your baby, but your budget won't allow it. You'd like to cut corners, but there are none left. It all seems impossible, so you continue down the same track.

But it doesn't have to be that way. Remember, if you never ask the question, you'll never find the answer. Ask yourself, "Do I want to stay home with my baby?" If the answer is yes, then open your mind and heart for possible solutions. Let your family and friends know what you want to do; ask for their ideas of how it might be possible. When Candice was two days away from returning to work after a maternity leave, she found the following notice on the bulletin board at church, "Couple wanted as resident caretakers of a small condominium complex, must be home during the day to take deliveries, one child okay." Within twenty days, Candice and Dave had moved in, and, in exchange for their work, they received an apartment that was better than what they were living in. Candice stays home with the baby and Dave goes to work. Keep the possibility open and ask for what you need.

ℛEST IN THE AFTERGLOW

he days of hanging the baby upside down and whacking his bottom after birth are happily behind us. Medical professionals have recognized what mothers have always known—that our babies' first impression of the world leaves a lasting impact on their delicate psyches. It doesn't take an expert to understand that lying with your baby on your chest, having skin-to-skin contact is a sweeter and more reassuring welcome than a trip to a plastic bassinet.

Following labor, you're worn out, yet more awake than you've ever been. Waves of ecstasy, relief, amazement, and wonder ripple through your body. There is nothing for you to do now; there's no place to go; you've reach your destination. You've been preparing heart and soul for this meeting. This is the sweetest of meetings; take all the time you need. In all your dreams, you couldn't imagine how moved you'd be at seeing this fresh soul, and there she is, lying on your belly. There will be a rush of activity around you, but don't pay it any mind—let the nurses, doctor, and assistants take care of the details. Your job is to connect to the beautiful one in front of you.

Your newly arrived baby with all his baby body parts is a marvel to behold. Go ahead and check to see if all his parts are in place, and count his tiny fingers and toes. He'll look wrinkled, gooey, and bloody, but don't be alarmed, that's normal. His miniature body is so appealing, even though his little head is squished from the tight journey. You can tell by the look on your husband's face that he's not merely proud, he's swept away.

A deep satisfaction settles in, and you know that this is what it's all about. The three of you are entwined in a circle of energy—the afterglow of birth. Wrapped in a safety net of love, you're meeting each other on a deeper and higher dimension, at the soul level where all time is no more. It's a dear, gratifying, exalted connection. You won't need words to describe it; you'll be showing it through tears. Your baby is the center of your world. You won't be able to take your eyes off her. You're falling in love with a fresh, indescribable love like you've never known before.

In the hospital, your baby will be quickly weighed, measured, and given an Apgar evaluation. The nurses and your husband will fuss over you—let them. It will seem as though you've entered the twilight zone. It's like running a marathon—you've been through a physical trial, and, when you cross the finish line, you can't believe you did it. You can barely catch your breath, and you're higher than a kite. You deserve the glory of this completion—you've done it, and your baby is here. You can rest assured in the afterglow.

Now my belly is as noble as my heart.

—Gabriela Mistral,
on being pregnant

ADDRESS THE BABY BLUES

hildbearing lasts much longer than the nine months of pregnancy. The child-bearing process begins when you decide you want to have a child; continues through pregnancy, labor, and delivery; and ends with post-partum. The minute labor ends, you'll enter the postpartum phase and your body will begin the recovery from birth. Your hormones are in flux, emotions are shaky, and there's a letdown. Postpartum lasts until your baby is sleeping through the night, which can be as long as a year.

Gone, unfortunately, are the days when a new mother stayed in the hospital for a good rest, to be pampered by nurses. These days, the maximum stay is two to three days, and many insurance plans are getting moms home in twenty-four hours. Suddenly, instead of having a relaxed transition, you're thrust into a hectic baby routine. Your body is trying to recover while you're getting to know your baby and perhaps dealing with your other children.

Be prepared to feel strange. The physical recovery from birth, combined with the rebalancing of hormones, throws your body out of kilter. This, coupled with lack of sleep and your new role, can throw you into overload. Almost all women have some form of the baby blues, which can run the gamut from tearfulness, irritability, guilt, regret, confusion, sadness, and fear to, in a small minority of cases, panic attacks and a prolonged depression requiring treatment. A first time mother, Marie said, "I had a storybook picture in my head of sitting with my husband, adoring our beautiful, happy baby. But it didn't happen. Infants require more work than I expected. The baby cried, I cried. I'd get to sleep, the baby would wake up. I couldn't even take a shower until my husband got home. I wasn't enjoying my baby, and I felt bad."

You might not enjoy the first couple of months as much as you think. But with some advance preparations, you'll know what action to take:

1. If the blues come upon you, don't isolate yourself. Talk to your to husband, doctor, midwife, or nurse. Ask your girlfriends who have children how they've dealt with the blues. Call them and let them know how you're feeling. Remember, most mothers feel depressed to some degree, so don't be embarrassed.

2. Take time for yourself. You'll cope much better if you have time to be by yourself a little each day. When your baby is sleeping, drop what you're doing and rest. Hang a "do not disturb" sign on the front door. Ask a neighbor or friend to watch your baby so you can at least walk around the block, work in the garden, go to the gym, or do whatever makes you feel better.

3. Lighten up and don't be hard on yourself. If there's laundry in the middle of the room, walk around it. Eventually everything will get done.

4. You don't have to know everything about parenting this week; you'll grow into it.

5. Take baby steps. Don't push yourself. Remind yourself that you need recovery time for your body and emotions to get bask to normal.

With a baby less than a week old, you're probably feeling ambivalent and scared. Your baby cries and you haven't a clue what to do. Remember, crying is one way a baby communicates, if your baby is crying that doesn't mean he doesn't love you or that you are inadequate. It only means that she is trying to communicate. Crying is a way for you to communicate also. Crying is good. Tears are a release, a sign that too much has built up in you. You've been through so much this last year—bliss, pain, disappointments, ecstasy. Your heart is so full. Tears come out of too-muchness—you've been keeping so much inside. If you need to cry day and night—go ahead. Let tears flow, and you'll feel unburdened.

Include Grandparents

randparents are a natural resource that no child should have to go without—including them from the beginning of your pregnancy strengthens the familial bond. Grandparents offer a second pair of hands, which come in handy when you're in the homestretch and can't bend over anymore. After the baby's here, Grandma and Grandpa can keep track of your roving toddler while you bathe the baby. Support from grandparents makes pregnancy more manageable and the adjustment to a baby in the house less hair raising. The first months can be highly stressful; the demands of a new baby can frazzle even the most experienced parent. Watering the wilting plants you've ignored since your bout with morning sickness, vacuuming, changing the beds, and straightening the kitchen—let your parents and inlaws give you a respite from household chores while you recuperate.

Allow grandparents to celebrate with you. Marce invited both grandmothers for the ultrasound. When the doctor reassured them everything was normal and announced, "You're having a boy," the grandparents were all ready to baby-sit. Jean bought Emma one of the finest strollers made—the kind she would have liked for her babies but couldn't afford; now it gives her joy to do it for her granddaughter. While grandparents may provide financial bonuses, gifts aren't the only advantages. Cally was a colicky baby and cried for two months, and, when Leilah felt she was about to lose it, she'd call her mom, who gladly stepped in.

The role of a grandparent in a baby's life is deep and far reaching, going well beyond gifts and free baby-sitting. Grandparents delight in grandchildren in ways that only a person with so much life experience can. Grandparents shower their grandchildren with unconditional love; they tend to be more patient and make fewer demands than parents do. First time parents are often anxious, overprotective, and hypervigilant, hovering around the baby, concerned with ever burp and whimper. Grandparents have done it before and are able to take parenting in stride. They get a kick out of watching their grandchildren, which also benefits your children. Seeing how much Grandma and Grandpa enjoy them builds confidence and self-esteem. Grandparents have practical skills, too. They've probably mastered bathing, feeding, diapering, rocking, and burping and are thrilled to relieve you of these tasks.

If you're leery about involving your parents or in-laws because you've heard horror stories of grandparents taking over, consider clearly expressing ways you'd like them to contribute. "My mom enjoys little babies and my mother-in-law likes older kids, so I divided the tasks accordingly. Mom rocks and feeds, while my mother-in-law takes my preschooler to the park." Another way to include grandparents is to ask them to record your family history. When Marilyn learned that her daughter-in-law was pregnant, she began a grandparent journal, recording stories from her childhood. When her grandchild is old enough, she'll pass this keepsake on.

Grandparents are the best ally for your child. While you may not agree with how they raised you, there's no need to focus on those differences now. They probably learned and mellowed as they watched you. This is an opportunity for you to reconnect in a loving and warm way. Rise above resentments and overlook the small stuff.

This is the time to consider forgiveness. Divine love may be perfect, but human love is not. Forgiveness means you accept your mother or father as she or he is. Real forgiveness has no judgment. You don't need to say, "You've done wrong, and I forgive you." Forgiveness means you accept your mother and your father as they are with no grudge, no grumbling. Arriving at the state of forgiveness requires spiritual work on your part. We all have wounds from our childhood; poking them keeps them from healing. You don't need to forget what has happened to you, just live this present moment.

Wonder

Stop for an instant, alone and still. Pushing the furniture of your mind aside, listen for the silence. Nothing between you and an unborn soul. You can't describe it, yet in this ephemeral gap, you catch a glimpse of the divine link between all creatures, and you begin to understand what it means to be a mother.

When your baby moved inside your body, did you not feel the inter-relationship between your souls, the sun, and the moon? Have you not felt life pouring from everywhere? There are many mundane tasks that go with being a mother, yet there's much more to it. Happy is the child who has a happy mother.

ᛈONDER BABIES

ou can't be pregnant without thinking about babies—cute, cuddly, roly-poly, rollicking babies. You'll spot them wherever you go, and you'll notice that even if you are in a cantankerous mood, you're more agreeable when a baby is near. Babies have a magical sweetness about them—big tough men have been known to play peek-a-boo and coo around them. Babies are curious, they like to touch and taste everything; watching one discover his hands and feet is amusing. Have you noticed that a toothless smile gives you such a boost that you're baffled how you've lived so long without it? You can't ignore a baby's cry; it grabs your complete attention; you stop whatever you're doing to find out what's the matter.

Babies are a sweet gift, a treasure, a soul in an irresistible package. In the presence of babies your heart melts, your mind clears, your face lights up, time slows down, and you're instantly transported to the land of Right Now. Babies speak a universal language; they're ambassadors of goodwill, ready to unite us across race, gender, and all other barriers. Babies are illuminated; perhaps it's the fresh halo above them.

Stand at a nursery window and take a peek at the bundles in receiving blankets. Just a few hours old, wearing pink and blue caps, and already you catch a glimpse of tiny temperaments. No babies are alike. Their fingerprints, tufts of hair, and personalities are all unique. Nothing tugs at your heart like a baby.

As you think about babies, ponder these questions: Who are these little ones? Where did they come from? Why are they here? What do you imagine they're thinking and feeling? In a very short while, a very special soul is coming your way; what will he be like? What will be her deepest fear, her greatest wish? What will her soul's task be?

Babies are human and spiritual beings, not our possessions. (By the way, the word *being* comes from the Sanskrit word *bhu* which means "that which grows.") We're entrusted to be their caretakers, their guardians, appointed as protectors to watch over them as they grow. Babies grow at their own pace, so it's not a good idea to force them. Babies are helpless; they have to take what you give; they depend on you for everything. They are at your mercy. Babies are cute, and they require tremendous energy—you must make a great effort. And by taking good care of your baby, you'll learn to be patient, to persevere, and to be kind. How you treat your baby when you're worn out, cranky, and exhausted shows the stuff *you* are made of.

Babies are God's messengers, reminding us of the continuous sweet circle of life. They haven't been corrupted. Looking at a baby, you catch a glimpse of your original face. If you haven't looked at yours or your husband's baby pictures recently, now is a good time. Jane collected baby pictures of each member of her and her husband's family, made a collage, and hung it in a large frame in the baby's room. A family tree of pictures showing the resemblance through the generations reminds them of their connection with each other.

Your baby carries the fragrance of you, but he has his own divine destiny. Babies are the blessing. Of all the wonders in the world, babies are the best.

> *The sweetest flowers in all the world—A baby's hands.*
>
> —Swinburne

WILLINGLY EMBRACE
THE TRANSFORMATION

 xpecting a baby changes your life in epic proportions. You know it's true. As your waist starts to thicken you can feel it. As your tummy protrudes you can see it. Soon it's obvious to everyone. You're having a baby! Strangers pat your tummy; acquaintances tell you labor horror stories; your mother takes gleeful pleasure in knowing someday soon, you'll get a dose of what you put her through. A couple of months ago you were oblivious to the magnitude of your journey; now you're beginning to comprehend the windfall. And so as you diligently prepare, you patiently wait.

Your waiting is filled with wonder. You're as eager as you've ever been—there's excitement in the air. As your body changes, you begin to grasp that as your baby grows within you, you're evolving, too—there's a divine transformation taking place. As the nine months pass, you're becoming a mother. From now on, your life is eternally linked with another's. Fortunately, this is a gradual process, in which you become acquainted with the little person while you adjust to the new you.

Pregnancy and the birth of your baby changes life for you and your husband forever. Your relationship takes on a new dimension. You're becoming parents! As your hips broaden, your vision expands, and you'll detect subtle transformation daily. Once you went out on Friday night; now you'd rather cozy in. Once you thought as a couple, now you're thinking as a family. Suzie said, "I knew things had changed when I went shopping for shoes and ended up in the baby department buying sleepers with snaps." Perhaps for first time, you're interested in talking to your mother about how she felt when she had you. Before your pregnancy, baby showers felt like obligations; now you're intrigued by the stimulating conversation. Your childless friends seem dull.

The transformation is deep and ongoing. As you begin to feel and look pregnant, you may try to keep your weight in check, then finally you surrender and let nature run its course. You realize you can't control everything, which is an understanding that comes in oh-so-handy when your newborn's finally here. You feel connected to the great circle of life. In a very real way, your body has been given over to something beyond yourself—you have become a vessel, a container for new life. It's the quintessential feminine act—to be the container for creativity, to provide the void, the womb out of which something new is born. By experiencing this miracle at its deepest level, you are in touch with your eternal feminine self.

Physically, your body is revamped, your emotions run amok, and your awareness is turning inward. "I felt a subtle presence within me, a faint sensation," said Amy about her pregnancy. "No matter what I was doing, I was in tune with my baby." Every day now you'll probably touch your tummy and check in with your baby.

When your tummy's covered in stretch marks and you're wondering if its worth it, suddenly you notice that your fingernails are longer and your hair more luxurious. You're reminded once again that you're in the middle of a grand metamorphosis. One day you're freaking out about labor and doubting if you'll be a good mother; the next day you're feeling feminine and proud to be a woman. You're committed—there's no backing out now—so, as millions of women have done before you, you face each surprise with courage and conviction. You're vital and things are happening.

I was slowly taking on the dimensions of a chest of drawers.

—Maria Augusta Trapp,
on being pregnant

ℒet Yourself Be Radiant

hroughout the ages, it's been said that a woman is the most beautiful when she's pregnant—a fresh glow surrounds her; she has a happy, healthy look. You're a woman and it shows. Your body is lovely, feminine, rounded, full, pulsating with life, and you feel sensuous. Yet when you look in the mirror, you don't always see the beauty, because you're so accustomed to looking for the flaws. But if you soften your gaze and pause, you'll see a gentle radiance—something is shining through.

Beauty is not merely physical; beauty is, at its core, spiritual—the shining through of the soul. Unless the spiritual dimension of your beauty shows, mounds and pounds of beauty potions won't do you much good. And unless you appreciate your spiritual beauty, you'll always compare yourself to others and end up feeling let down and lesser than, unfulfilled and frustrated. Letting yourself be radiant is about seeing the depth of your beauty and knowing its source. It's not painted on from the outside; it's illuminated from your center, dances from your eyes, explodes from your heart.

The image of a frumpy pregnant woman who has to hide at home in a voluminous dress so no one sees her condition is a thing of the past. Looking and feeling your best, enjoying your pregnancy, celebrating life, stepping in tune with the divine is a more fun, lively, satisfying way to go through pregnancy. What makes you feel attractive? It's probably a combination of many things: your vitality, enthusiasm, bubbling energy, and positive attitude, as well as your clothes, hair, and makeup.

To see your inner beauty, incorporate a beauty meditation into your routine. Set aside ten to twenty minutes. Play soothing music. Using dim lighting or candles, sit in front of a full-length mirror and gaze into your reflection. Making no judgments, stare into your eyes without blinking. Even if tears come, don't look away. The face in the mirror will begin to change; you'll see different faces, all belong to you. You might get scared, but keep on looking. Eventually, you'll look past your face and see your radiant inner splendid self.

Physical beauty routines are fun, too, as long as you keep them in their proper perspective. Again, there are no "have tos." Some women love ruffles and bows; others wouldn't be caught dead in them. Some prefer accentuating their form, others feel uncomfortable in too-tight clothes. Do what feels right for you. Judy, a law professor, wanted to maintain her dignified persona at work and didn't want too much attention drawn to her body as she lectured. She found five simple dresses and rotated them with scarves and jewelry. On the other hand, Barbara, a freelance writer, was proud of her big belly and wore tights and form fitting tops.

If this is your first pregnancy, you probably won't need any maternity clothes for three months, but if you've had children before, you're likely to show sooner. I asked an expectant mother, who has a three-year-old toddler and is known for her head-turning good looks, how she managed to dress so chic. Her trade secrets: black leggings with colorful silky tunic tops, oversized cotton T-shirts with shorts, one black A-line dress (she had hers made so she could find a comfortable fabric), a good pair of wedgy black shoes, and something feminine and soft to sleep in. She also recommends wearing big choker necklaces with all your outfits and, if you have short hair, earrings. Your fingernails will grow longer, so paint them your favorite shade of pink or red.

What you wear truly doesn't matter as long as you do it with panache. It's your energy and verve that makes you attractive. Clothes and cosmetics are fun, but the best beauty secret is in the joy of being pregnant—the radiance comes from within. Enjoy the sensuousness of your rounded body and let your pleasure show.

RESPECT YOUR AMBIVALENCE

Pregnancy is a complicated experience—it's not all joy and bliss. Deep within your heart, many conflicting thoughts and feelings collide as you prepare for your new life as a mother. No matter how overjoyed you are to be having a baby, there might be feelings of regret, confusion, and sorrow. You want this baby with all your heart, and even so you have misgivings: Did I make the right decision? Maybe I don't have enough patience to be a mother. Will my partner still find me attractive when my waist is gone? You may be troubled with second thoughts: I don't think I'm ready for a baby. There's bewilderment as you see the new you emerge and perhaps a bit of resignation as the former you melts away. Doubts, worries, and spoken and unspoken fears bubbling under the surface make you wonder if you're normal or going crazy.

Martha said, "I feel as if I am both celebrating and mourning. I want this baby, yet am sad about curtailing the career that I worked so hard on. My identity is changing from executive to mother, and, even though I am sure of my choice, I feel twinges of doubt. Up until three months ago, I was focused on advancing my career. Now my focus is shifting, my colleagues treat me differently, and I'm not sure I like it. I was excited to become a mother and disoriented at the same time."

How will your life change when you're a mother? You read books and think about it daily; you want to be ready. Some days you're confident you can handle it all, other days you aren't quite sure. It's natural to quiver at the significance of your responsibility. Diana told me, "I don't talk much about motherhood to my husband, but I talk a lot about it with my woman friends, and I wonder if I'll be a good mom. Sometimes I get very scared." People say to me 'you'll be a great mother,' but I don't know it."

Conflicting thoughts and feelings are natural, so there's no need to feel guilty, avoid your feelings, or push them away. When you're doubting your ability to be a mother or you're feeling guilty because you're missing your nonpregnant freedom, do something special for yourself. Go for a walk. When you're out of doors, you can't stay in a dark mood for long. Sitting by a lake or a stream is a renewal for body, mind, and spirit. You may need to cry. Crying releases pressure and pent-up energy, and, as you let your thoughts and feelings wash through you, you'll find within yourself an inner strength to accept these troubling moments without getting stuck in them.

As a mother-to-be, you are becoming more aware of your connection to all living things, and that stirs within you a deepened commitment to making a contribution to the human family to which we all belong. You may ask yourself how can you make a difference. You might feel sensitive about lots of things. Jayne said, "I was teary and felt alone. I needed reassurance, but even my husband, who was really understanding, didn't understand. I wanted to be cheerful, but I was depressed off and on and took everything he said as criticism."

Your independence and freedom seems to vanish. The line between you and your unborn child blurs, and you wonder if your identity will be lost forever. This can be unnerving. You can't fathom it all at once. You know a baby will change your life forever, but you can only guess at how this bundle of joy will impact your life.

Feeling vulnerable, sensitive, shaky, weepy, baffled, slightly crazed, or plagued by misgivings is natural at any stage of your pregnancy. When this happens, remind yourself that other mothers-to-be have similar doubts, so you're not alone. And remind yourself that you *will* do a wonderful job because you want to and are committed to being a good mother. You'll do whatever it takes, including seeking outside help if you need it. And by reaching out, you'll be plugged in to an abundant supply of love and assistance.

COMPLAIN, COMPLAIN

here are no typical days when you're expecting—everything is out of kilter, and there are plenty of adjustments to be made. Right away, you're startled by the potent smell of your everyday surroundings. Certain odors take on a pungency, and a whiff of a once-favorite aroma can suddenly send you gagging from the room. You might develop such an aversion to certain smells that you avoid going to your favorite coffee shop because the smell of fresh coffee makes your nose twitch, or you avoid going to the movies because the stench of popcorn makes you retch. Folks who have never been pregnant might accuse you of being picky or whiny, but pregnancy complaints are justifiable, so let yourself protest now and then.

There will be weeks in the beginning and again toward the end when it will seem as though you spend most of your days scouting for the nearest bathroom. Before you leave the house, you have to plot out exactly where the rest stops are, because when a pregnant women has to pee, there is no time for delay. A mom-to-be with a developed sense of the ridiculous told me she was going to sell maps of all the clean potty stops between her house and the mall, because no pregnant woman can make it ten minutes without peeing.

Pregnancy is inconvenient and awkward in more ways than one. There are those necessary yet annoying doctor's office visits. Now you weigh in every time. You feel fat and doubt your ability to lose even one pound, let alone thirty, after what your body's going through. The nurse assures you that you'll do fine, especially if you exercise. Exercise? Isn't it enough that you're already chasing a two-year-old toddler around? And after the baby comes, who will have time for exercise? What you need is a nanny; then maybe you could take a walk, or better yet get some sleep, since you've had insomnia for months.

Patty didn't complain during her first pregnancy, because everything was exciting, but with her second it was a different situation. "I hated going to the doctor and having all the medical stuff done. I'd complain to Jeff and he'd rub my back and say, 'I wish I could do this for you.' Then I felt better."

Complaining is endemic to pregnancy. When I asked a classroom of expectant moms whether or not they complained, they answered, "Yes, all the time!" and when I asked them to explain, this is what they said: "I'm fearless now about speaking up." "Sometimes I complain to myself, but I do feel better if someone will listen." "I'm much more vocal now about whatever bugs me." "If you can't complain when you're pregnant, when can you?"

One mom said, "My protective mother nature is emerging. I don't want to raise my child to be a doormat. So I feel I have to set the example even now. Plus, if I don't let it out, I think my baby would be more nervous or high strung. Perhaps that's a superstition, but it's how I feel."

Complaining is not all bad—it is a good tension release, and often allows you to get to the bottom of what's bothering you so that you can find a possible solution. Of course, with pregnancy, sometimes the solution might be just a day of commiserating about all those little annoyances. So, feel free to unload your troubles, but be careful that you don't equate complaining with a need for your husband, doctor, or friends to fix it. Let them console you with a nod or a hug. If all you need is for your husband to commiserate about the little stuff, ask him just to listen. After all, most of the complaints of pregnancy are little unsolvable annoyances that simply must be lived through.

Keep breathing.

—Sophie Tucker

Ask for Guidance From Your Girlfriends

rom the first moment you decide to bring a baby into the world, you're committing yourself to nine months of bearing a child, hours of take-your-breath-away labor, and years of being unselfishly available through every phase of your child's life. As your innocent baby becomes a roving toddler, then seemingly overnight turns into a hormone-crazed teenager, you've appointed yourself to watch over the evolution of a person—his or her body, mind, and spirit. It's a grand responsibility for which you'll surely need divine guidance! For a minimum of the next two decades, you'll have lots of questions, and, when the answers seem to elude you, there's always fabulous guidance readily available—just a phone call away—from your friends who are already mothers.

There's a cord of camaraderie among women who are pregnant or have had children. Expecting a baby is an initiation of sorts into a society of sisters who know what you're going through—they've been there and done that—and who are more than willing to help you out. Strangers become instant advisors, experienced moms welcome you into their fellowship, eagerly sharing their cures for stretch marks and morning sickness, enthusiastically standing by, reassuring you when you're alarmed by the black line running down your abdomen, or comforting you when the doctor recommends a cesarean.

Becoming a mother opens the door to relationships with other women who not only enrich your life, but can share valuable information that comes in handy. Other pregnant woman can understand when your husband can't, and, share a point of view that you might have overlooked. When you need to know what to expect during any aspect of your pregnancy, nothing is better than talking with someone who has had the same experience. Olivia knew she was scheduled for a cesarean and got valuable information when she talked with a woman who'd had a cesarean with her first child, but was able to have a vaginal birth with her second. It's comforting to know that you are part of a great circle of women who have been through what you're going through. Just knowing that others have been through childbirth in less desirable conditions gives you a spurt of strength.

Emily bought every pregnancy book off the shelf, checked out every childbirth video from the library, and dedicated herself to becoming informed. She says, "I couldn't remember most of what I read because it was too clinical, too complicated, or too calm. And the videos freaked me out. So when I had a question or an experience I wanted to process, I'd call my girlfriend, the mother of three, and she answered me in straight talk and gave me down-to-earth advice that I could actually use."

When Liza's husband announced he did not want to "catch" the baby in the delivery room, it was her girlfriend who convinced her not to worry, because many men who turn out to be good fathers faint at the sight of bodily fluids. And when Morgan saw hair growing in places she'd never had hair, it wasn't her doctor, her mother, or her husband she confided in—it was a friend who was also expecting.

As necessary as doctors are, no matter how wonderful your husband is, or how supportive your mother can be, there are some queasy, embarrassing, shocking, funny pregnancy situations that only an enlightened girlfriend can tackle. Pregnancy and childbirth are momentous occasions when you'll surely need women friends; after all, pregnancy is a woman's domain. So when you're in a panic because you know the weight you've gained is more than baby, or you're dazed by all the medical terminology—call your girlfriend and find out what she thinks.

RENEW YOUR RELATIONSHIP

ou and your partner are probably awestruck at the thought of your new baby and the responsibilities of parenting that are tumbling down on you faster than you expected. Perhaps you're speechless when you listen for the first time to the swishing thumping sound of your baby's heartbeat. Maybe you're caught off guard by the magnitude of your emotions, and jarred by the realization that the three of you are eternally linked.

The love expressed between a mother and father for their unborn child is powerful. It's the foundation of your family. By bringing a child into the world, you're pledging to be conscientious, faithful, and devoted to one another and to your child. Since how you treat your spouse will affect your baby, each of you must be willing to do whatever it takes to make sure your relationship with one another is solid. Your lives are now permanently interwoven, and, now more than ever, you must grow in loyalty to one another.

The loyalty between two people who love their baby and are willing to stand by each other through thick and thin is premium. Loyalty, one of the greatest qualities in a relationship, is the fragrance of love. Pregnancy and childbirth will bring new challenges and stresses to your relationship, but, by being steadfast in your allegiance to one another and, faithful in your word and action, you'll add a richness to your life that wasn't there before.

Together you've created life and you're redefining your relationship to include a joint promise to put the needs of your baby above your own. Your pledge to take care of this baby and honor your partner is more important than the immediate gratification of your or your partner's needs. Particularly in the first months, your baby's needs will often come between you, and you're likely to feel neglected by your spouse, but when you respond out of your commitment to your partner, then your baby reaps the security of a loving family. There will be days when you'll think about running away from it all, but out of loyalty, you'll put your own needs on the back burner and stay. What you gain is a deeper relationship and a more secure family life.

Take your approaching parenthood earnestly and recognize that you are parenting partners. Perhaps you might want to even have a private ceremony—just between the two of you—to renew your commitment to one another and vow to work together on behalf of your child, no matter what. Together you might write a ceremony and ask your minister, rabbi, or trusted friend to bless your union, your child, and your added commitment. To write a simple ceremony, talk about how you met and fell in love. Write about what you've shared and how you've grown. Think about your decision to have a child, and what it means to be parenting partners. Make a verbal promise to jointly be there for your baby. Just as your wedding rings are symbols of your never-ending love, you might choose a symbol to remind you of your parenting commitment: Plant a tree to symbolize the dedication that caring for a life requires; make a braid of different colored ribbons (one to symbolize each of you), and hang it over the nursery door or on a wall in your bedroom. Seeing the tree or braid will remind you of the tie connecting all of you.

Strive for honesty in your communication. Talk over parenting issues. See if you can come up with a mutual philosophy that will guide your daily decisions. There are all kinds of wonderful parenting resources. Don't be afraid to use them now. Be supportive and try not to criticize and control. Show compassion for each other. Your baby needs you to treat each other well.

Allow for Moodiness

You're having a baby and you're ecstatic—well sometimes you're ecstatic. Other times you're cranky, tearful, feisty, lonely, frustrated, testy, forlorn, whacked out, and miserable. Your hormones are on overdrive, and you are experiencing mood swings as wide as the Grand Canyon.

In the first trimester, tears flow like water over Niagara Falls, and anger erupts so unexpectedly that you start thinking of yourself as Mt. Momma. Your husband squeezes the toothpaste in the middle and you're convinced he doesn't care about you as much as he used to; after all, he should know by now that you prefer your tube neat. You scold him about his negligence, and, as soon as the words are out of your mouth, you're so embarrassed by your petty outburst that you wouldn't blame him if he never forgave you. You're dramatic, hysterical, and sentimental. You cry over baby blankets and weep buckets of tears over phone commercials. One week you're sleeping so much people wonder if you've slipped into a coma. The next week you have so much energy, you're taking on causes and ready to become an activist. "When I see adults even looking sternly at children, I want to report them to the authorities," said Donna. You can also be impulsive and irrational. Ginger signed a contract with a photography studio for eighteen years of family portraits, and Rene scheduled interviews with gymnastics schools that take six year olds to find the perfect match for her as-yet-unborn baby.

When Lisa told Donald she was expecting, she was so disappointed in his response she accused him of being "an insensitive creep." When she cried, "I knew you didn't really want this baby," he was baffled. When Lily asked Geoff how she looked in her new maternity jeans, he answered, "Do you like them?" He knew he'd made a big mistake when she locked herself in the bathroom, but he had no clue how to redeem himself.

If you haven't figured it out by now, moodiness goes hand in hand with pregnancy. You'll feel better faster if you acknowledge that you're feeling cantankerous. Tell your husband that moodiness is normal, especially during the first three months, and ask him not to take it personally if you sometimes lash out or cry uncontrollably. And then try not to hold him responsible for your ups and downs. Give him kindly instructions as to what would be helpful if you throw yourself on the bed and can't stop crying. Agree on a word like *crabgrass* or *petunia* to signal when one of you needs a time out. A time out is a safety net to keep your moods from affecting your judgment. You both agree to leave one another alone for at least twenty minutes. According to the latest research, it takes that long for the hormones to calm down. After a timeout, you can come back together and discuss whatever the issue is more calmly.

Even when hassled, bedraggled, full of self-pity, and moaning, try not allow your negativism to take over. Otherwise, you'll fall into a pit of depression and won't be able to lift yourself out. Accept your unreasonable behavior—yes, here I am again, convinced my husband is a jerk—but don't give it so much energy that it becomes a way of life.

The child-soul is an ever-bubbling fountain in the world of humanity.

—Friedrich Froebel

GIVE YOURSELF PERMISSION TO BE NEEDFUL

Her sweet, old fashioned, French grandmother advised Annie, "Just because you get sick or tired when you're pregnant, don't deny your husband." A modern women, Annie thought about it for a minute and hollered, "No, no, I'm the one who's pregnant—he shouldn't deny me!" That evening she shared her grandmother's advice with her easygoing husband, Rick. From then on, "Don't deny me" became their secret code meaning *she* wanted *his* affection. When she says, "Please don't deny me," he doesn't question her. He's good natured about it and understands that she's in need of a dose of undivided attention, which *he* gives and *she* soaks up.

Now that you're pregnant, you'll probably be like Annie and feel more dependent on your husband. Even though you've been independent all your life, when you're carrying his baby you're more needful. Not needy, but needful. (Needy means you're impoverished and unable to care for yourself, which you're not; needful means you require something, which, of course, you sometimes do.)

As a mother-to-be, you're switching from the independent role of taking care of yourself to a mutually dependent role in which your baby relies on you and your husband for everything. It's an awesome responsibility. Hard work is required, including days when your pregnancy is nothing more than heartburn, stretch marks, endless trips to the bathroom, and an aching back. On those days you'll need a hug, a kiss, some cuddling, and a listening ear.

Like Annie, you might find a playful way to let your husband know you need his healing attention. Read him Annie's story and tell him that there are days when the only thing that's helpful is his arms around you. Wrapped in his strong embrace you can let go of your worries. It's moments like this, when you think you can't go on another minute, that his arms are the only place you feel safe. Nothing soothes like your husband's arms holding you.

If you're feeling needful and your husband isn't near, there are other things that work. There's a old gospel hymn, "Take it to the Lord in Prayer," which I heard my grandmother sing when I was a child. To this day, when I'm troubled, I can hear her voice singing it, reminding me of where I need to turn. During my pregnancy, when I didn't know what I needed and couldn't give it to myself if I did know, I took the song's advice. When you can't put your finger on what is troubling you but know you're troubled because you can feel it in your bones, telling God about it is the best way to go. My grandmother took everything to the Lord in prayer. She said no burden was too small to share. In situations when you haven't a clue as to what you need, the cure is found not in the asking, but rather in the telling.

Even if you are exhausted and disoriented from labor and medications, looking at the creature who has been living inside of you for all this time will be the closest thing to seeing God that life can provide without the help of a burning bush or parting sea.

—Vicki Iovine

RECEIVE THE HELP THAT'S GIVEN

hen Jacqueline was expecting triplets, her type-A personality kicked in over-drive, and she was overtaken with super-mommy syndrome. She made a list of 112 projects she wanted done before her due date and pro-ceeded to check them off. The list was endless: She bought a year's sup-ply of greeting cards and addressed them in advance, she set about organizing every nook and cranny and made sure socks were folded, bulbs planted, and wills and insur-ance policies updated. She'd checked off fifty-seven items before she was diagnosed with toxemia and ordered to slow way down. "Is it necessary to have everything done?" her best friend asked. "Yes!" she answered. "Then you'd better ask for help," her friend replied.

In this shaky predicament, Jacqueline was forced to take a personal inventory. Assigning tasks and working as a team was not difficult for Jacqueline in her job as supervisor of the city's summer fair, but, in her personal life, it was an entirely differ-ent matter. Would it be kosher to ask her friends for assistance? Could she muster up the nerve to receive help?

First she called on relatives, who were pleased to be included. Great-grandmother and a great aunt took over the garden, dried the herbs, and made the jam. A cousin sewed and hung the curtains, her husband and his brother rearranged furniture and lined a closet with shelves. Her dad researched, purchased, and assembled a triplet baby stroller. By the time Ashley, Abigail, and Adam (weighing in at under four pounds) arrived, she'd organized a team of "changer, rocker, feeder" baby volunteers. "Ask for help," she advises, "and don't turn down what's freely offered."

While you may not be carrying triplets or want friends reorganizing your kitchen, there will be days when you'll feel drained and depleted. You'll get tired of being pregnant, tried of making decisions, and wish someone would take care of you. Even though caring for a family is what you always planned, secretly there are days when you feel helpless. Even though you can't wait to be a mommy, when you feel like a dependent baby yourself, it's time to practice the art of give and take.

God sends many earthly angels to get you over the troublesome spots. Some come as your husband, some as your friends, and others come as strangers just when you need a little something special. So take the help of any preferential treatment that comes your way—it's probably an earth angel giving it. If someone offers you a seat on the bus, take it. If relatives and friends want to wait on you, don't be a martyr by saying, "I can do it myself." You're already doing plenty; now is definitely the time to let yourself be coddled.

As a mother, you're in a state of constant giving; once in a while you need to receive. Receiving for many women is more difficult than giving. When you give, you have the upper hand—you're in charge, you feel good, and your ego is enhanced. But when you receive love, you can't have the upper hand. Receiving is threatening to your ego, because through the act of receiving your ego starts disappearing.

There is a Buddhist saying: *Do not turn away what is given you*. If you turn away, you miss the opportunity to let the walls around your heart melt. For love to flow freely between two souls, you must both give and receive. Sometimes you're the giver, and sometimes you're the receiver. When a gift of help is given, you give back by graciously receiving. If you do all the giving, no one else gets a chance.

Forget not that your body contains the whole of existence.

—Gopal

$\mathcal{B}$E IN HARMONY WITH YOUR BABY

very expectant mother I spoke with sensed that she and her baby were in tune with one another's body rhythms and feelings. Researchers as far back as the 1930s found that maternal attitudes and moods could leave a lasting imprint on the unborn child. Studies seem to indicate that from about six months, the fetus can see, hear, and taste. There's speculation that the unborn child's emotional life is closely connected to his mother's. Several midwives told me that not every worry or anxiety will impact the unborn baby, but a consistent pattern of upset can leave a scar or tendency on the unborn child.

Studies show that long before birth, mother and baby are beginning to respond to each other. It makes sense that bonding happens first through your body rhythms. If you're thinking everything will be all right, you're likely to feel happy. And when you feel happy, your body responds with relaxed muscles, you move at an easygoing pace, and your body is flooded with endorphins, which produce a natural high. Conversely, when you are anxious or upset, your muscles tense and your body is flooded with stress hormones. Just as oxygen, food, and nourishment pass through your body, the fetus senses your mood and absorbs the vibrations.

So what can you do at the end of a hard day when you're uptight? Your husband is in bed with the flu and you still have dinner to cook and a toddler to bathe. You carry on and do what you must do, of course. But you do it in a new way, with a gentle manner and loving attitude. You can do your chores grudgingly and make yourself and everyone miserable, or you can do what needs to be done with a smile. Freaking out, slamming the doors, or rushing, huffing, and puffing won't change anything except make you miserable. Smiling and talking softly will help the crankiness dissolve. You can cut corners. Open a can of soup, jump in the bath with the baby, unplug the phone, and turn out the lights. You've always got options. Whatever you do, don't condemn yourself for getting uptight. Every pregnant woman does. It's much worse to be like some women, who don't even know when they're upset. You're ahead when you recognize your moods and body rhythms, because then you can begin taking positive steps to change your reactions. When you do, you've found the key to living in harmony.

By observing the subtle body rhythms in your baby, you have an opportunity to begin to get in sync. Your unborn child is aware of what's going on around him; he's sensitive and remembers; he's trying to communicate with you. Some moms know what's going on with their babies by the way they kick. Some dads play and talk with their babies by getting very close to the mom's belly and saying hello. If the baby's awake when dad pushes on mom's belly, the baby might kick back.

Before birth and after, babies have varying sleep patterns and levels of alertness. A tuned-in mom can recognize the times when her baby is in deep or light sleep, or awake and active. While you probably can't wake up a deeply sleeping fetus, there are periods when the baby's awake that she's hypersensitive to input and loud noises. Baby Gigi for example, danced and rolled when mom played rock and quieted down with a piano lullaby.

One study even found that babies move in rhythm to their mother's speech. An unborn baby doesn't understand the meaning of your words, but does respond to the tone in your voice. You can help your baby relax and feel loved by talking tenderly. I was told the story of a woman who regularly sang a special lullaby to her baby. After the baby was born, if he was crying and heard the melody, he immediately calmed down.

Never doubt that your baby wants to get your attention. While this fact may not be scientifically proven, expectant moms know it to be true: Unborn babies want your undivided attention, because just as you settle down for a good night's sleep, they get active and start kicking.

ℒavish Yourself in Laughter

 f you've made "to do" lists of what you needed to get done by Thursday, then misplaced it or forgot to read it over, you're not alone. Many expectant mothers tell me they're forgetful, absentminded, and suffer from what one woman called pregnancy "insanity. I'd showed up on the wrong day for doctor's appointments so often they started calling twice to remind me."

At any stage of pregnancy, you're likely to act deranged and suffer from illogical thinking. "This feels like permanent PMS. I go to the grocery store, buy five cans of talcum powder and forget the bread," laments Rene. Whether your pregnancy dementia is due to hormonal changes, busier schedules, or sleep deprivation, the reasons don't matter as much as how you handle it. Laughter is probably the least harmful option.

Before your nine months is up, you'll get dozens of tips from relatives and strangers—everything from the silly to the downright outlandish. If you want twins sit under a weeping willow; if you want a boy, sleep with a sharp knife under your mattress; if a baby girl is your heart's desire, put a rusty iron skillet under your side of the bed. Sleep under a full moon and your baby will be lively and smart. For a head full of hair, drink plenty of carrot juice; if you want your baby to have dimples, sleep with your cheek on a button; and if you want an easy labor (who doesn't?), eat fish on Sunday.

There are plenty of laughable pregnancy moments. There's a joke in almost everything, even gas: "My husband calls me his gaseous girl," laughs Louise.

There is considerable research on the benefits of laughter. Laughing has healthy effects on the cardiovascular system and stimulates the brain to produce catecholamine—the alertness hormone. Have you noticed how awake you feel after you've had a good laugh? By laughing, you can shift your focus from what's troubling you to appreciation for the lighter side (ha! ha!) of your pregnancy situation. When you're able to step back, you gain a new attitude, which lets you relax and enjoy even the most annoying situations.

You may not think it's funny when your father-in-law teasingly asks, "What's cooking?" or "Are you done yet?" but you can turn it around with a wink, a smile, and thumbs up. By viewing life with a little detachment, you can let the inconsequential slide and have more fun. Emotionally you'll feel better when you do. Laughing with your husband, friends, relatives, and strangers is an embrace of love, compassion, and understanding for our human foibles. Approaching life with a lighthearted view, you can see the bigger picture—the cosmic angle that puts our problems in perspective.

And if that doesn't convince you, perhaps this will. Laughter has been found to have a link to pain reduction because of the hormones released when you're laughing. Besides—when you're laughing you're distracted from what's bothering you and at least for a minute or so you feel fine. I don't know of anyone who has laughed all the way through labor, but perhaps it's possible with a highly developed sense of the absurd.

A mother of wisdom is full of laughter. She knows her role is important, but she approaches pregnancy with a lighthearted reverence and a twinkle in her eye. She's playful while she's ranting and raving about the cost of delivery, and whistles while she practices mashing and grinding vegetables so she'll be an expert at making baby food long before her little one is ready for solids. She sees the ridiculous lengths she'll go to in order to try to paint her toenails, but doesn't let it get her down. She shows respect for human nature by laughing at her own foibles. And if she's brave enough to look at her pregnant belly while standing naked in front of the mirror, she knows she's certifiably hardy enough to be a mother.

INDULGE THE UNPREGNANT YOU

hen you're tired of being "with child" and can no longer see your feet while standing in a shower, if you're having second thoughts and can't remember why you wanted to be a mother in the first place, these are all symptoms that you're in desperate need of a pregnancy distraction. When you find yourself crying for no reason—cranky, depressed, or downright ornery—it's an indication that you need to break free and do something on a whim. The best antidote to the "What have I done?" blues is to do something silly and spontaneous so that you can forget for at least one afternoon that you're a mother in waiting. Even though every cell of your body is pregnant, there's still an "unpregnant you" that needs attention once in a while too.

The unpregnant you is the woman you used to be or wish you were right now. She's always available to you whenever you can't see your way clear. She has her own identity and knows what she needs to make herself feel centered. To make connection with the unpregnant you, ask yourself this question: What did I like to do before I was pregnant that I haven't done in quite a while? When you hear the answer, that's exactly what you need to do. And if the answer is "I don't know," it means you haven't concentrated on yourself enough lately.

Reija, the mother of an eight month old, told me, "If I had known how little time I was going to have for myself after she was born, I would have seen a lot of movies." Kennedy said, "I would have taken longer baths and bought a crossword puzzle book." Cheryl said, "I would have had breakfast in bed with my husband a few more times." And Angie said, "I would have built a darkroom."

Think of it this way, if you're sensible all the time, you're going to get rather boring. It's not only just okay to indulge in your favorite pastimes, it's required—because that's what makes you an interesting and unique person. Maybe you like to play bingo, bridge, or golf. Maybe you'd like to go to a matinee or while away the hours writing letters from your favorite coffee shop. Perhaps there are some friends you haven't seen since you've been so busy. You could make arrangements to get together or, better yet, drop in.

If you get a sudden impulse to take your shoes off and walk barefoot, don't think about, just do it. If you get an urge to leave in the middle of the sermon, do that too. If silliness overtakes you, enjoy yourself. Don't squelch your natural tendencies to be young at heart and free.

Even though you are pregnant twenty-four hours of the day, it doesn't have to be your sole focus. The unpregnant you will be there no matter how many children you have. She deserves attention too. Perhaps you've overlooked your talents lately; maybe you've pushed aside your dream to write a short story, sing in the choir, or throw a pot. Perhaps you've used the "I'm pregnant" plea and let your authentic self be smothered with obligations and excuses.

Giving birth and raising a child is deeply gratifying, that's for sure, but it's not the entire picture. You can be a wonderful mother and develop yourself! But I'm not sure you can be a wonderful woman *without* developing yourself. Letting your talents dry up serves no purpose whatsoever. It makes you one-dimensional! As we nurture our children, I think we must also nurture our talents.

It takes at least twenty-one years to raise a child, but it is done one minute at a time. Likewise, it takes many years to cultivate your dreams, but they, too, are achieved one minute at a time. Give your unpregnant self ten minutes each day to nurture your talents—in twenty-one years, you will have achieved a lot.

Surround Yourself with Light

ince expecting a baby is intrinsically spiritual, this is not the time to neglect yourself spiritually. Feeling a connection to the divine is as natural as making sure you're eating well. Your spiritual connection—be it prayer, meditation, spending time out of doors, or another daily spiritual practice—will bring you comfort and help neutralize your deepest fears. Because pregnancy is such an experience of loss of control over your body, your appearance, and, to a great extent, the outcome itself, it forces you into faith in the beneficence of the universe and into trust for a good outcome.

Toni highly recommends going into nature to feel the connection between yourself and the rest of life. She says, "When I was pregnant, I felt like Mother Earth. I could feel my connection to the cycle of life. I felt closer to my pets, the land, my roses. Every time I saw a blue heron or a red-tail hawk, I'd cry."

Everyone needs something different. Lana had a recurring dream that her baby was born with no hands. It upset her tremendously, and even though the amnio confirmed she was carrying a healthy baby, she was haunted by the dream. Together we designed a personalized visualization for her daily use. She began each day by visualizing her and her baby surrounded in a warm, loving protective light. She used the affirmation, "I'm carrying a healthy baby boy and I'm enjoying my pregnancy," and repeated it several times daily. At night she said a prayer and asked for guidance. She fell asleep visualizing being gently rocked and surrounded by light. Using this technique, she reprogrammed her mind and broke the grip of fear. If you are apprehensive, you can do the same thing.

Visualizing is a method of putting positive thoughts into mental images. There is considerable scientific research that proves that visualization and relaxation produce bodily responses, such as lowering heartbeat and blood pressure. Athletes use visualization to improve their performance, and it's often used in childbirth to support the mother in a positive and peaceful birth.

Surrounding yourself with a protective, warm, loving light will help you in all kinds of unknown or tense situations. You can create your own visualization to use during medical exams and tests, as well as in throes of labor. It works best, however, if you practice before you need it. Use a favorite visualization for five minutes each morning and evening. Sit or lie down in a comfortable place, where you won't be disturbed by the phone or by kids barging in. You might not even need silence or privacy. While riding on the bus to and from work, Melanie imagines herself pushing her baby in a stroller on a sunny afternoon, and it works so well folks wonder why she's always smiling. Choose whatever mental picture helps you feel calm and serene. It might be a waterfall, a meadow, a gentle breeze, or a flower. You know best what image works for you. Concentrate on that image as you allow your body to completely relax.

Affirmations are positive selftalk in short concise sentences. Design two or three to use with your visualization such as: I'm enjoying my baby; My body is beautiful and working so well; I'm able to move easily through each contraction. Each morning as you pop a prenatal vitamin, surround yourself with light and know that you and your baby are protected.

You know more than you think you do.

—Opening words of *Baby & Child Care* by Dr. Benjamin Spock

JOIN A CLASS

ou're going to attend pregnancy school, which is both fun and intimidating. One twenty-four-year-old father-to-be told me that when he walked into the classroom and saw all the other parents, he realized he was no longer playing house. "I was the father and I wanted to run away." He got used to the classes and they helped him, but it was difficult for him because not only was he getting pregnancy and delivery information, he was struggling with his new identity and responsibility, and he felt as though he had no one to talk it over with. My experience is that this is not an uncommon reaction for many first-time fathers and mothers. Fathers, however, don't have as much opportunity to talk these issues through and may find it harder to express their feelings. Be sensitive to this, and, if your husband seems preoccupied or irritable the night you attend your class, this may be the reason. You can approach the subject gently by saying, "This is an adjustment for us."

Nicolette gave birth at a maternity clinic in France and had no childbirth classes. She subscribes to the Odent philosophy that women know exactly how to give birth and do best without instructions. Most other women disagree and find classes more helpful. Classes prepare you so that when you're going through it you won't need to think much at all, but can go forward on automatic pilot.

First you'll start to understand the vocabulary. Pregnancy talk is a new language. There are words and terms you've never heard or used before and will only use again if you or a friend is pregnant. From Kegel exercises (pushups for the bladder), to quickening, Apgar scores, and vernix, you're going to get an education. From Bradley to Lamaze, you'll have your pick of different childbirth philosophies.

DeeDee thinks, "The greatest thing about childbirth class is my husband got to hear about bothersome afflictions from someone other than me. I had carpal tunnel, and hearing that it's a common pregnancy syndrome helped us." Clark and Mindy made lasting friendships with other pillow-carrying parents in their class and go to yearly reunions along with their babies. Mindy said when the instructor asked, "How many people will have children present at the birth?" Clark coughed and nearly fell off his chair when five couples said they would have children present.

At class, you'll watch videos of births. The same young man told me he was in shock and couldn't look directly at the first video he saw. But he wanted to be brave, so he didn't let anyone know how afraid he felt. In the end he was glad they showed several, because when he attended his son's birth, "I felt as if I'd become a real man." His wife told me he was a real trooper.

Marianne went into early labor just before class, with only one session to go. The instructor called for a wheelchair and took her to the triage section, where it was confirmed that she'd be admitted. In her mind, she'd prepared for a long labor, but in only four hours and fifty-five minutes, she and Allen were looking at a puffy-eyed, pink, scrawny, five-pound ten-ounce baby girl. Marianne told me, "She wasn't the Gerber baby, but she was ours, and we got so much pleasure holding her and learning what she needed." Allen and Marianne were the guest instructors at the final childbirth class.

In class, you'll see that labor is gut-wrenchingly hard, and delivery has queasy and traumatic aspects. Remind yourself that this enormous physical achievement has spiritual and emotional significance, and you will rise to the occasion. Thinking in this way brings a sacredness to everyday life. One last thought for you to consider as you watch childbirth videos: I think it's important to bring a quality of reverence to your watching, because when you are a witness to a birth, you are standing on holy territory.

SCHEDULE TIME FOR SECLUSION

y the thirty-ninth week, you'll probably be moaning, "I'm permanently pregnant." By week forty, you'll be screaming, "Get this baby out!" With all the stories you've been told and all the advice you've been given, you might get stuck on information overload. While being the center of attention can be wonderful, don't be alarmed if you feel inclined to avoid well wishers. When you're immobilized by the immensity of impending parenthood, when folks start asking, "Haven't you had that baby yet?" and you sarcastically answer, "Yes, I had it last week," a mini-retreat is called for.

Instead of forcing yourself to be cheerful and keep going, schedule some time for seclusion. You've had enough conversation about bodily functions; now what you need is privacy. Wrap up in your favorite blanket and don't answer the phone. Hibernate and let yourself be quiet. You might not be able to lie dormant for nine months, but you can hibernate for at least an hour or two. In the final weeks and days of pregnancy, every mother-to-be gains from a dose of solitude. You need the salve of silence.

Seclusion is the basic requirement for discovering the Divine, for nurturing your soul, for finding refuge from a chaotic day. Unplug the phone, turn off the television and the stereo, and let your thoughts drop and subside; listen for silence. It reverberates through every cell with healing tones. Sitting in silence, you come to know truth. Silence, like the vastness of desert, has its special beauty. It's boundless and undisturbed; peace prevails there. In the silence, you expand and know yourself in an unspoken, undefined way.

One of the most challenging aspects of caring for a newborn is finding a moment to be with yourself. If you can bathe with silence now and be alone you can call on those satisfying memories when you are swamped with too much togetherness. In seclusion, you learn that you don't want to hurry the process—you learn to rely on serenity. Face these seemingly endless last weeks by taking them one day or one hour at a time. Curl up and read a book of uplifting quotes. Take your toddlers to a sitter and hide out in your favorite room. Wear your most comfy sweats and don't put on makeup. Marlana's favorite way to hibernate was to lock herself in her basement and paint for an entire afternoon. Do nothing in the middle of the day. Private moments for contemplation can be the most creative part of your week.

Sit quietly, and, as you touch your belly, focus on your breathing. Say to yourself: "The time for my baby to be born is nearing; this is natural process." Go for a short, slow walk, and, as you take each step, notice the beauty all around; let yourself feel in harmony with nature and know your body is in good working order. When you feel impatient, remember God is watching over you, no need to rush or hurry. Pregnancy doesn't go on forever: Labor *will* begin.

Some days you won't know what to do, so just wing it.

The seasoned mothers I talked with told me they wished they had taken it slower during their pregnancy because the stage of "living on the baby's schedule" comes very soon. Before you know it, your life seems consumed with diapers. I asked Irene, age eighty-three, mother of five, grandmother of ten, and great-grandmother of seven, if she had advice for expectant mothers. "Learn to knit," she said. "Make something pretty and let the God take care of the rest." She reminded me that the creative project grounds us in the knowledge that life is moving under a heavenly plan.

Whenever you're feeling anxious, give yourself silence and your heart will fill with peace. The more you find silence, the better you will feel. With daily practice of soaking in the silence, without any doing on your part, you will come to feel and know that peace has been established.

GET READY FOR LABOR

ver the last months, you've looked at your expanding torso in the mirror, stashed crackers by the bed, bought a larger bra, propped yourself up with pillows, and tried to imagine labor pains stronger than your worse menstrual cramps, but you couldn't quite grasp it. Then the day you've been waiting for arrives. You have mild cramps, a dull backache followed by a stop-in-your-tracks contraction. Your water breaks; you call your obstetrician, grab your husband and a pre-packed suitcase, and, as you head out the door, you hear the faint voices of friends reminding you that "labor pains are indescribable." You're wheeled into the birthing center, aware there's no turning back, you steady yourself for the hours ahead. The contractions get closer, grow more intense, and you cross your fingers, hoping to maintain a smidgen of decorum. As the hours tick away, you no longer care. This is when you'll be glad you did these two preparatory meditations:

1. The silence of the womb. Early in your pregnancy—before your belly is too large, sit on the floor and collapse as if you are a baby in your mother's womb. Sit this way and soon you will start feeling that you want to put your head on the floor. Take the womb posture and immediately you will feel silence—the silence of the womb. As you get larger, you can also curl up in a fetal position under a blanket and remain there doing nothing. The more practice you have, the less frightened you'll be.

2. Shades of blue. Meditate by looking softly at something blue. Blue, violet, and purple are the most soothing of colors, because they're the color of the sky, of tranquility, of silence, of stillness, of peace, and of relaxation. Whenever you are really relaxed, notice how you suddenly see an aura of blue luminosity—it's so pervasive you can feel it. Surrounding yourself with shades of blue and purple will help you relax. Bring something in a shade of blue to the labor room. Choose an object that is especially

pleasing to you—blue lightbulbs, a blue silk scarf to drape on the bed or hang from the wall, a light blue pillow case, amethyst crystals or beads in a clear vase near the bed.

I don't want to scare you, but let's be honest, labor's not for wimps. But don't worry if you are a wimp before you start—you won't be when you're done. Yes, labor hurts, but it doesn't last forever. I've heard of women who didn't want to hear about the pain or were so nervous about giving birth that they shielded themselves from labor stories and were deprived of helpful information. When it comes to going through labor, ignorance is not bliss. That's one of the reasons why the first time is the most difficult. Second-time mothers are less tense and able to move with the pain. When you know what to expect, you can prepare yourself and be more in control. So be willing to hear other women's stories. But be careful not to expect your experience to be exactly the same. Every birth is different.

Remember, you're not alone. Your body's natural painkillers, endorphins, are released at about two hundred times normal levels during labor, and you can always have an epidural if you need it. Your labor nurse, doctor, or midwife will be close by, watching over you, making sure you and your baby are safe. It's also such a comfort to have your husband nearby, offering ice-chips and back rubs, but don't be surprised if when it's over, your husband is exhausted too. Several studies have found that fathers at the end of labor are almost as fatigued as mothers.

No matter how happy you are for this day, when you're in the middle of it, you'll want it to be over. "I was ready to go," laughed Fran, "and then I had a few killer pains and thought, just maybe I could put it off for a week." Trust in your body, respond to its lead, and know that each contraction brings you closer to your baby. Repeat your labor mantra: "This won't last forever, this won't last forever" or "I am doing it, I'm doing it." Lean into the pain. Have faith in yourself and surrender to power of this moment—other life experiences will seem trivial in comparison.

Immerse Yourself in Stillness

ou might be surprised to learn that your newborn is alert and wide-eyed for many hours following birth. We can only imagine what it's like to leave your nine-month home and, crawl slowly through a tunnel to push out into a big new world. Does she wonder where she is? Is she scared? When you think of it this way, you want to make the transition as gentle as possible. You want her to be safe. Your baby is beside you—slowly she opens her eyes, and stares at you. Her first impression of the world is you, so soften your gaze, look kindly and friendly, and she'll keep looking. "When Nicholas was one hour old, we were fascinated with one another; we couldn't take our eyes off him and he didn't look away either. Our souls merged."

Perhaps it's in the stillness of this eye-to-eye meeting that you begin to understand that even though you're separate beings now, in a way you're actually more connected. Perhaps it's in the stillness that you give your unspoken promise to be this child's mother. You grasp how much you're needed, and you tremble. The desire to be a good mother swells, and, although you don't know what all that entails, you vow to do whatever it takes. You take a silent oath to love, protect, and watch over this precious being. Perhaps it's in the stillness that you give your commitment to be available to your child forever.

Fathers who participate in this special twenty-four hours of stillness develop the same strong attachment. They give their unspoken commitment to be a father, to love, cherish, guide, and provide, and, although they, too, are uncertain, they pledge to do their very best.

Five hours after delivery, four-year-old Thad, two-year-old Ellie, and Fred climbed into Rita's bed and took a nap, but not newborn Timothy; he was wide awake and looking. He was checking out his family. You've been through the birth of the baby, now you're experiencing the birth of a family. In the sacred stillness of these moments you fall into loving unity. With your family present you might say a soft prayer of union and affirmation, something like this: "This our family. We come together to help each other, to laugh and grow. Thank you for each unique member (say each person's name)—we are a beautiful bunch."

This is precious, delicate time; there won't be another like it. If the nurse comes, tell her you want to be quiet. There's plenty of time for details and chatting later, this gazing time is what's important—mom, dad, and baby are bonding. Your lives are linked; your souls have joined; the angels must be singing.

If newborns could remember and speak, they would emerge from the womb carrying tales as wondrous as Homer's.

—Anonymous

REJOICE AND WELCOME YOUR BABY

 fter you've delivered and are on the way home, you have a high-level appointment—a date with a baby, so put a mommy, daddy, baby rendezvous first on your agenda. You're going to have goose bumps as big as baseballs, so settle back, soak up the fun, and rejoice. You all deserve the glory.

You'll sense how trusting your baby is and how much she needs you. Even second-time moms are surprised how quickly their mother lioness instinct takes over. You know you'll go to any length to protect him; from now on, you want the best for him and you'll move heaven and earth to see that he gets it. Already you're biased and you admit it, but, even if you weren't, you're convinced that anyone with any intelligence can see this is a one-of-a-kind baby. His ears and nose could win a cuteness prize. Talk softly to your baby and notice how she moves her head toward you; she'll recognize your voice right away. I've seen videotapes of hour-old babies turning their heads ever so slightly toward familiar voices.

She's so sweet. Look at her with kindness and she'll look back. Keep your baby close to your body and softly touch her puckered skin. Babies need to be touched; they like to cuddle and nuzzle. They feel comforted next to you. Some moms like to talk directly to their baby, others communicate through gentle touch and singing. Say what's in your heart. Tell him, "Hi baby, I'm so glad you're here." Sing or hum a lullaby. When you get to your house, say something like, "This is where we live, please come in."

I was so enthralled with Amanda that when she was one week old, I forced my relatives—her grandparents, aunts, uncles, and cousin—to play a game that went like this. Each person in turn would say "I like Amanda because . . ." and would repeat what was previously said and add their own reasons. My relatives played and teased me, but I couldn't help myself, a love cloud hung over my head and I couldn't stop bragging.

The silly game became a family birthday tradition, and, ever since then, whenever we celebrate anyone's birthday, we play it. Amanda's embarrassed, but secretly it must mean something to her because she still, at nineteen, indulges me. I think other folks like it, too, because whenever we celebrate a friend's or relative's birthday, someone asks if we're going to play the game, and of course we do right away.

Plan a welcoming ritual. A welcoming ritual is a way of expressing your love and delight at having a new member in your family. A simple ritual brings your undivided awareness to the specialness of the moment, sealing it in your heart and memory. Simple songs, poems, a moment of silence, or a prayer will mark this day as a family holy day, which indeed it is. Include your spouse, children, grandparents, or friends if you'd like. Manuel and Angel put a bouquet of baby roses and candles in the baby's room and, along with grandparents and friends, hummed a song of welcome as Manuel played the guitar, "We welcome you into our hearts today. We love you. We love you little one. We welcome you into our hearts today. We welcome you home." Do whatever feels right to you to celebrate this miraculous birth!

The ideal mother, like the ideal marriage, is fiction.

—Milton Sapirstein

$\mathscr{S}$HARE YOUR CHILDBIRTH STORY

andice worked in an office with two expecting coworkers. She soon found out what you probably already know—that every mother-to-be has a pregnancy story to tell. "We talked every day about nausea, stretch marks, sex, food, and labor. During our lunch hour we'd shop for baby clothes. We did our jobs, but our primary interest was our condition."

The history of pregnancy and childbirth clearly shows that "birthing babies" has always been women's territory. Up until the 1800s, birth was an event completely managed by women. A female midwife and friends would comfort and reassure the mother through the process. After the birth, they would stay two to three weeks, running the household while the new mother recuperated. It was referred to as "lying in," meaning the new mom stayed in bed, being cared for by friends. Friends gathered to do whatever was needed.

A vital aspect of the lying-in period was sharing experience and telling stories. It wasn't until male doctors took over the delivery that the social aspect of birth was pushed to the background, and women's role in the process diminished. Now once again there's a growing recognition that women are best suited to help each other.

Women help each other most by sharing their stories. "I like to talk about my pregnancy—it helps me realize I'm not crazy," said Susan. "When I share my childbirth story, I have a sense of accomplishment," said Simone. "I'm proud of myself. I did it. I made it through." Telling your story is cathartic. It's a release of emotional tension after an intense and monumental experience. By telling your story, you restore your spirit and join the community of women throughout the ages.

Almost immediately after labor, you'll start telling all the details. You'll need to talk. In fact, nurses studying obstetrics are told to listen carefully to new moms' stories. "I couldn't wait to call my friends, and I couldn't stop talking," remembered Simone. "They understood and listened to the details." Telling your story replenishes your energy, so find as many ways and seize every chance to tell it. Many hospitals have support groups for new mothers. Frequently, they provide child care during the meetings. Churches also frequently sponsor new moms' groups—if there is not one in your area, consider starting one with the women you met in your childbirth class.

You have a pregnancy story and soon you'll have a childbirth tale. Tell your story, but a word of caution. Don't tell your childbirth story to a pregnant woman unless she asks. A pregnant lady needs pregnant stories; childbirth stories are for later.

Every birth is a getting to know.

—Paul Claudel

PLEDGE YOURSELF TO PARENTING

he title Mommy or Daddy is a distinguished and noble epithet—bestowed upon you by an innocent child—that you earn through years of hard work. That's because giving birth to your baby does not make you a parent. Parenting is a way of life, a skill (you'll have lots of years to practice), and an art (you'll develop great understanding and compassion) that is acquired over time, based on your positive attitude and your unselfish behavior, and through your diligence. To become a parent means you're dedicated to your children and the plight of children everywhere—it's your long-term dedication that secures the title.

Parenting means going out of your way to give your child the very best start in life. Parenting is a prolonged commitment of your energy, love, and all the mental and emotional resources you can assemble for the benefit of your child. Now that you're expecting, parenting is becoming your sacred obligation. Although you may have lots of theories about parenting, the only thing you know for sure is that when you bring a baby into the world, you give your unspoken assurance that you'll be actively involved in the well-being of the upcoming generation.

Instant parenting doesn't work. Leaving it up to others doesn't qualify you; doing whatever it takes does. It takes courage to be a conscientious, committed parent, willing to put yourself on the back burner, not with resentment but out of love for your baby. No one forces you to give birth and become a parent; it's your choice. Once you make that choice, it's your responsibility to evolve into a parent of integrity and compassion.

For most of us, parenting doesn't come naturally. To be a parent, you must endure months of sleepless nights and mounds of smelly diapers; you must survive days when nothing you planned gets done because you're spending the day picking up toys, making beds, packing lunches, and chauffeuring. Parenting is full of countless hard choices. When you take the pledge to parent, you promise to learn all that you can about parenting. If you have no skills or knowledge, you immediately take a parenting class, read parenting books, or seek counseling.

Jean reminisced as she rocked her new granddaughter, "It's astounding that such a tiny baby can require so much work yet fill your life with so much love." Your parenting routine begins with a diaper bag and continues as you acquire an enormous bag of skills. Parenting is an all consuming venture—twenty-four hours a day for the next twenty-one years or more. It's not for the faint of heart, because halfhearted parenting won't do.

Pledge yourself to parenting and follow through. You'll receive many blessings if you do. Shelby and David agree, "The love for our children is as immense as the ocean." There is no greater work the Almighty has given.

I lost everything in the postnatal depression.

—Erma Bombeck

Accentuate the Love

 eing pregnant, giving birth, and caring for a child are all experiences of love. When you look into the eyes of your beloved baby, if you allow your heart to melt, you'll become possessed by a love for your baby that is greater than you—it consumes you, satisfies your longings, brings contentment and exhilaration.

"I can remember when Craig was born and they brought this gangly skinny baby with a red face and a black eye to me," said Jean. "He looked so helpless and needy. When I looked into his face, I felt a protective urge, and all the doubts and worries that I had before disappeared. I said to him, 'You may be a baby only a mother could love, but I do and will protect you and be there for you as long as you need me.' Of course, worries and doubts reappeared and continue to this day, but I do my best to keep that feeling of love in all my decisions related to his upbringing."

When you love your baby, you not only help him grow, but yourself as well. For the love you give enhances you, too. Your baby is the mirror, the reflection of love back to you. Love for your baby doesn't mean you have to get lost in the shuffle; rather it is the love that allows all that you are to emerge. Love transforms you into a mother, observing, allowing, accepting.

Make a commitment to love. A baby has great potential for love—it is up to you to let that love flower. When love for your baby is playful, sincere but not serious, then your heart runneth over with joy, and you are born anew.

Love allows you to be authentic, to become sensitive, to feel more, laugh more, cry more. It's through the small things, the mundane things, that you gain the larger view. Love makes it possible to put yourself in your children's shoes before making decisions that impact them. Love mixed with a splash of laughter added to your daily routine makes even the dullest day sparkle. Having a baby is definitely a peak experience, but loving your child daily, weekly, yearly is the essence of life. Love is the source, and love is the end. Fifty years from now, when you stand with some distance to look at back at your life, what will matter most is that you loved your children well.

> *Unfortunately, it is the rule rather than the exception that babies arrive at least a few days late. Nevertheless, when the forty weeks have expired and the baby has still not showed up, it is almost impossible not to feel hopping mad.*
>
> —Audrey Hull

Prayers of Affirmation

When said with arms outstretched toward the heavens, prayers produce a sense of well-being, insights, and other victories:

I am thankful for life growing inside my body,
for my husband, my family, my friends.

I ask you, the highest power in the universe
to take my self-doubt away;
to fill me with appreciation
for myself and how far I've come.

What shall I do? I'm confused.
Can I love enough to be a mother? Here I am.
Show me, guide me, watch over me, protect me.
Let me know the way.

As gold passing through the fire
is shined to the highest radiance;
You polish my soul with pregnancy challenges
so I become a mother filled
with wisdom, light, and love.

I've decided to have this test, but I'm frightened.

    I want everything to be okay.

    Hold my hand, cradle my heart, stand by my side.

    Be with the staff, give them the skill, give me the courage.

....

I waddle, my back hurts; I can't bend over anymore.

    Get me over these speed bumps, Lord.

    I want to feel pretty, laugh, and have fun!

    Let me eat chocolate, drink tea, and make love.

    I need to dance, paint a picture,

    sleep a sound night's sleep.

....

My body is beautiful and working so well; I'm able to move easily through
each contraction.

....

My mother—although she did the very best she knew how to do—was not perfect. I wanted her to be but, of course, she was human also. She probably took
the best of what her mother gave her, improved on it, and gave it to me. Guide
me to do the same. Let me take the best of her, improve on it, and pass it on
to my baby. Let my baby do the same.

Any day now I'm going to go into labor. I'm excited. I've been told I can do it. Bless me with sweet assurance that it's true.

....

May our little one be blessed with love, health, and spirit. May we, the parents, be blessed with wisdom, strength, and generosity of soul. As we get to know each other and settle in, bless our family with gentle words and loving smiles.

....

We welcome you into our hearts today. We love you. We love you, little one. We welcome you into our hearts today. We welcome you home.

....

This is our family. We come together to help each other, to laugh and grow. Thank you for each unique member (say each person's name)——. We are a beautiful bunch!

....

I believe that the force that moves the heavens also moves in me.

Acknowledgments

Bringing a book into the world is a little like pregnancy, labor, and parenting. There are many months of preparation, thrills, and taxing work. Then when the book is finally out, it takes a whole team to guide and watch over it. Fortunately, I have brilliant Conari Press coaches: Brenda Knight gave me the original inspiration; Mary Jane Ryan, my writing mentor, understands what I'm struggling to say, and, when I want to give up, she encourages me take a deep breath and keep going; Ame Beanland assisted with the perfect title and ensures exquisite packaging. The rest of the company works faithfully in the background, cheering "my baby" on. I'm glad they're by my side.

Thank you, dear Cheryl, for believing I could do it when I was in the last days of hard labor trying to deliver this book.

And sweet blessings for my Marie, who understands my soul.

OTHER BOOKS TO GUIDE YOU

You can find lots of name books. Here are two I liked reading: *The Ultimate Baby Name Book,* by the editors of *Consumer Guide; The Complete Book of Baby Names, Traditional and Modern,* by Hilary Spencer.

I recommend you give your husband a book about being a father. He might appreciate *The Keys to Becoming a Father,* by Wm. Sears, M.D., or *Fathering,* by Will Glennon.

A book about the emotional aspects of birth and recovery is *The Journey of Becoming a Mother,* by Laurie Kanyer. It gives guidelines for starting a new moms' support group in the back.

I really like the children's book, *Happy Birth Day!* by Robie H. Harris.

The Childwise Catalogue: A Consumers Guide to Buying the Safest and Best Products for Your Children, by Jack Gillis and Ellen R. Fise is worth looking at.

SOME NEAT STUFF FOR YOU...

Birth and Beyond. A lovely store in Seattle filled with books and products. Lyndsey Starkey is the owner and can get almost any book, music, or product you're looking for. She has lots of helpful things, including what I've listed below. Write or call for a catalogue: Birth and Beyond, 2610 E. Madison St., Seattle, WA 98122. (800) 348-4831.

Hot Sox. This "sox" which really isn't a sock feels wonderful draped across your shoulders and neck when tense. Use in labor along your abdomen and back. Order from 4469 Woodland Park Ave. N., Seattle, WA. (206) 633-4701 (or at Birth and Beyond).

The Rosado Sling for infants and toddlers. The niftiest baby carrier I've seen. For info write or call: 7749 16th Ave. SW, Seattle, WA. (206) 768-2658 (or at Birth and Beyond).

Teddy Toes. A blanket with feet. By Sisters 3. (206) 284-3404.

MUSIC

Linda Ronstadt's album, *Dedicated to the One I Love.*

Baby Scapes: Soothing Music for You and Your Baby, by Mars Lasar.

I also highly recommend that you get any version of *Pachelbel's Canon.* Ask your music store.

Conari Press, established in 1987, publishes books on topics ranging from spirituality and women's history to sexuality and personal growth. Our main goal is to publish quality books that will make a difference in people's lives—both how we feel about ourselves and how we relate to one another.

Our readers are our most important resource, and we value your input, suggestions, and ideas. We'd love to hear from you—after all, we are publishing books for you!

For a complete catalog or to get on our mailing list, please contact us at:

CONARI PRESS
2550 Ninth Street, Suite 101
Berkeley, CA 94710

800·685·9595   Fax 510·649·7190
e-mail: Conaripub@aol.com